Understanding
Goose

To Sherry
With love,
Jean

More Titles by the Author:

Jacob's Journey
My Morning Cup

Understanding
Goose

*For anyone who has felt
different, rejected or empty*

Jeanie Shaw

Understanding Goose
© 2011 Jeanie Shaw. All rights reserved

Printed in the United States of America

ISBN: 9781463689582

Cover design: Jennifer Maugel
Interior design: Thais Gloor
Back cover photo: Vanessa Embling

www.jeaniesjourneys.com

To my husband, Wyndham,
whose love for God, for me, for our family
and for others inspires me and calls me higher.
I love you with all my heart.

And to the loving memory of
Richard and Martha Whitehead

Contents

Acknowledgments

Thank you to my sister, Carolyn Harrell, for her many helpful suggestions; Elizabeth Thompson, for sharing her gift of editing; Sheila Jones, for her wise counsel; Sharon Metzger, for her keen attention to detail; Thais Gloor and Jen Maugel, for their artistic abilities; my cousin, Betty Smith, for snapping pictures of the real "Gator Goose"; Vanessa Embling, for shooting the back cover photo; the "Understanding Goose" workshop participants who urged me to write this book; my family, for encouraging me in this project; and my son, Jacob, for graciously letting me share some of our story.

Preface

"Necessity is the mother of invention" is an oft-used phrase. For me, this book was born out of sheer desperation. In 1998, our family welcomed a new son and brother into our hearts and home: Jacob Shaw, a bright-eyed boy whom we had fallen in love with on our visits to a Romanian orphanage. Though I had worked for several years with a benevolent organization helping orphans and displaced children, I felt ill equipped to help my preteen son (an orphan for twelve years) as he adjusted to a new culture, a new language and life in our family. Though I had asked lots of questions in preparation, attended seminars and read many books, nothing could have fully prepared me for what it would really be like to raise our new son. The goose pictured here atop tension wires, nesting on another bird's nest, poignantly depicts the beginning of my journey. I was experiencing a new beginning on a "borrowed nest" while precariously balanced amid charged tension wires!

As I learned more about adoption transitions, two things struck me. One was that issues common to adoption are also common to those who experience various types of loss and trauma. As a minister to women over the past thirty years, I have spent countless hours helping them navigate through losses, disappointments, abuse, divorce and various life disruptions and complications. While everyone processes these things individually these types of situations often seem to have a number of common ingredients.

The second is that without the Scriptures and a relationship with God (which secular teachings often avoid) we miss the most significant and crucial path to healing! Certainly many things I read along the way were beneficial. (It is my conviction that all things work better when based on principles that have their origins in God's word.) However helpful, these guides are incomplete when they don't use the Scriptures that call us to begin and/or deepen our relationship with God.

I began presenting this material in a workshop format using various movie clips to illustrate each of the issues presented. While I cannot duplicate the workshop's visual presentations in a book, I do pray that the message conveyed in these next few pages will help you on your journey toward emotional and spiritual healing. I hope you will take some time to work through the questions at the end of the book designed to guide you deeper into the topics. I encourage you to do this in a small group or with a trusted friend. May you find rest for your soul as you come to "understand Goose."

Understanding Goose
For Anyone Who Has Felt Different, Rejected or Empty

Gator Goose stood outside the large glass window staring at my dad, who was in the sunroom sitting in his favorite chair.

Moving the newspaper that had been strewn across his lap, and leaving his coffee cup, a stack of books, and cans of cashews, walnuts and peanuts piled beside the window, Dad looked back at the goose and stood up. It was now time for lunch, so Gator Goose proceeded with his daily routine, a routine he had been following for several years. Following my dad, the bird waddled the length of the house

to station himself outside the kitchen window, where he watched Dad eat lunch. Gator Goose repeated this exercise day after day, going from window to window as Dad moved throughout the house. When my dad went outside, Gator Goose stayed near him except for an occasional visit to the opaque green pond that was the focal point of the back yard. Gator Goose had earned his name from his eyes— one was orangish red, and the other was blue—the same colors as Dad's favorite football team, the Florida Gators.

All too soon, Dad's chair was empty. Years of diabetes proved too much for his heart, and his body wore out. Now

it was Gator's job to accompany my mother, who was feeling particularly lonely, from place to place. He faithfully followed her from one side of the house to the other, watching her, protecting her now that Dad could not. No one, not even the mailman, dared come between Gator Goose and my mother. With his hissing and flapping, he was prepared for a fight with anyone who might try. You can see his "prepared to protect mom" pose in the photo of him above.

My sisters and I never knew why this goose was so loyal to my parents. We surmised, since geese have mates for life, that he had lost his mate and was looking to my parents to fill the void.

Shortly after Dad's chair was vacant, cancer took my mother's life and now her chair was also left empty. Gator Goose was alone. There was no one else at home. What would he do?

Gator Goose had complete access to the wide, unending horizon of the sky where he could soar with other geese. He had limitless ability to swim, play, dive and do all things goosely in the pond right in his back yard. Yet instead of experiencing the wind beneath his wings, the splash of the water and the view of the  landscape from far above the earth, he was shackled to the invisible chains of the patio outside my parents' brick house...waddling back and forth day after day, seemingly in search of somewhere to belong.

Have you ever felt like Gator Goose? Do you sometimes feel sad and isolated and like you don't belong? Shackled instead of free?

So many of us have experienced or are currently enduring great pain in life. Have you ever felt different, like no one can understand you? Have you ever felt a deep, nagging sense of loss? Have you ever felt rejected and worthless? Have you ever felt ashamed or guilty? Have you ever had a hard time figuring out "who you really are?" Do you have a hard

time letting people really know you, afraid that if they did, they wouldn't accept you? Do you have a difficult time trusting others, often thinking they are out to hurt you? Do you feel the need to be in control?

If you answer yes to several of these questions, or if you know someone who struggles with these feelings, please read on.

Like Gator Goose, we can find ourselves feeling very alone in this world. Like the children's game of Duck, Duck, Goose, we can feel that we are singled out as the one who is different from everyone else.

You are not alone.

Take heart in knowing that you are not alone. Throughout history, men and women have felt isolated and tormented to various degrees. The Bible gives us insight into numerous men and women who can relate to Gator Goose, and to us.

In Luke 8:43, we meet a woman who had severe and chronic bleeding. Surely this woman felt she could never function normally around other people. Deemed by society as unclean and an outcast, her confidence was likely very low. Embarrassed and alone, she was desperate to get to Jesus, if only to touch his clothing. Could he take away her loneliness and despair?

A man with leprosy (Matthew 8:2) knew what it felt like to be rejected, never to be touched or hugged. He was not allowed to function near others, lest they catch this dreaded disease that devoured his own flesh. Was there hope to be found? Would Jesus really touch him?

The adulterous woman (John 8:3) was "caught in the act." Brought out in her nakedness to face the judgment and jeers of the crowd, she also came face-to-face with Jesus. The crowd wanted to stone her. Feeling dirty and ashamed, could she ever look her neighbors in the eye again? Was her life over? Would Jesus throw the first stone?

The man called Legion (Mark 5:2) was deemed out of his mind. He continually cut himself on tombstones and likely wished he was buried under one of them. Trapped in mental anguish, he only knew the darkness of life. Why would Jesus ever know him or notice him? Surely anyone else was a more worthy candidate for Jesus' attention.

These men and women from the New Testament give us several views into painful emotions we may have experienced. These very real people were desperate because of their pain. Where would they take it? Could anyone provide relief? Would anyone care? They chose to take their pain to a man who they heard had the power to heal and to change lives, a man who people said truly cared.

Jesus had compassion on them and healed them. He touched them, forgave them and gave them the power to change.

It took courage and openness for them to face their pain and take it to Jesus. It takes the same courage and vulnerability to face our pain and take it to Jesus. Sometimes, however, like the paralyzed man whose friends lowered him through the roof to get to Jesus (Mark 2:4), we also need others to encourage and help us find him.

In reality, pain may be a gift in disguise that leads to our healing as well as our ability to appreciate wellness. Individuals who have a physical disorder that desensitizes them to pain end up in many perilous situations.

Perhaps you haven't experienced such a painful history, but someone you love has. Understand that the window from which they view life will be different than yours. Take the time to try to understand them. This will take courage as well.

Jacob, my youngest son (he was 24 years old at time of printing), has helped me "understand Goose" in a deeper way. Jacob spent the first twelve years of his life in a cinder-block orphanage in Romania. He had never even seen a family, or anyone who really cared for him. Then he came to join our family of five.

He and I could not have come from backgrounds more diverse. I grew up in America with a family who loved me and loved each other. He grew up in a country that had recently been released from an oppressive dictatorship, and he was without a family and without love. Jacob and I have had to learn through many trials to understand and appreciate one another. It has been a difficult journey and learning curve for both of us. I am sure I can never really appreciate (no matter how hard I try) the intense challenges that he has faced. These differences have caused us both to experience many emotions in our relationship.

After several years spent feeling desperately discouraged, fearing that we might never understand each other, or even truly enjoy each other's company, I stand utterly amazed at the progress in our relationship! Jacob is my son *and* my friend.

If you are tempted to put this book down, thinking you can't relate to our situation, please take note: Adoption isn't the only experience that can cause you to feel out of place and misunderstood. Today's world is filled with dysfunctional relationships. Many, if not most, individuals are in some way touched by neglect, abuse, death, divorce, addiction, financial difficulties or health challenges. If you have not yet experienced one or more of these situations, statistics tell us that you will. Our increasingly wired, virtual-reality world further contributes to relational dysfunction that affects our ability to feel the warmth of human connection. This "disconnect" can take root in the core of our souls and leave us feeling lonely inside of ourselves even when surrounded by a crowd.

If you have ever felt different, alone or disconnected, I hope you will take heart and gain hope by reading this book.

The lessons presented here are about bringing your pain to one who understands, cares, and can heal you if you let him. Gather your courage to face your pain and take it to him, as difficult as that seems. Only then can you know and experience the God of compassion and all comfort:

> Praise be to the God and Father of our Lord Jesus Christ, the Father of compassion and the God of all comfort, who comforts us in all our troubles, so that we can comfort those in any trouble with the comfort we ourselves have received from God.
> (2 Corinthians 1:3–4)

As you read, my prayer is that you gain:

A greater understanding of yourself and why you do what you do and/or think the way you think. Most often there are underlying issues at the root of our actions and reactions. When we better understand those issues, we become more equipped to overcome them.

A deep comfort, knowing someone can really understand and relate to you.

The knowledge of how to gain the power to change through a real relationship with Jesus, the "Wonderful Counselor, Mighty God, Everlasting Father, Prince of Peace" (Isaiah 9:6).

A place to belong.

A confidence that you have something to offer others.

Jesus Understands

One of the most phenomenal traits geese possess is their connection to "home." Their desire to return to their birthplace every year is so strong that they will often fly up to 3,000 miles to get there. Dangers and difficulties will not deter them from taking this journey.[1,2]

While trying to understand the real and painful feelings of disconnection, researchers have often noted several "core issues of adoption." By raising these issues they sought to challenge traditional assumptions about adoption, specifically "the persistent notion that being adopted is not different from growing up in the family of origin."[3]

These issues include loss, rejection, shame and guilt, identity, intimacy, trust and control.

Can you relate to any of these?

Certainly, these wounds are not just confined to adoption, as you already know or will come to understand.

The wounds can leave us feeling like paper doll people that have been severed from the rest. What remains is the need for something deeper that can fill this "hole in our

1. Interestinganimals.net
2. National Geographic News, October 28, 2010
3. Rosvia and Silverstein, *Adoptive Families*, March/April 1999.

soul"—this longing to feel connected and at home.

Many articles and books have been written to help understand and manage the resulting consequences of these issues; author Nancy Verrier calls them a "primal wound" in her book by the same name.[4]

I have learned much from these writings and wish to commend them, not cast any disparagement on them. However, something is decisively missing in our world's attempts to heal this primal wound.

Can Jesus relate to "feeling different"?

What does Jesus have to do with the goose who felt rejected and alone? Can he relate to feeling different, out of place, misunderstood? And if so, why would that matter to me?

Jesus was with God before the creation of the world, and heaven was his home. The world truly was at his fingertips, for he was the agent of creation. Yet amazingly, he willingly left the absolute perfection of heaven and came

---

4. Nancy Verrier, *Primal Wound*, (Gateway Press, 1993).

to this created world. He began human life in a borrowed womb and was born in a borrowed stable among all kinds of barn animals. Jesus knows what it's like to feel different.

Whose child was he really? What was his last name? Was it Jesus Josephson, after his earthly father Joseph? Or, was it Jesus Godson, as the son of God? In the Scriptures, Jesus is called the Son of God by those around him:

> "Yes, Lord," she told him, "I believe that you are the Christ, the *Son of God,* who was to come into the world." (John 11:27, emphasis added)

He calls himself the Son of Man:

> Jesus replied, "The hour has come for the *Son of Man* to be glorified." (John 12:23, emphasis added)

Where and to whom did Jesus belong?

Jesus arrived here via an "extra-dimensional" adoption or surrogacy that we cannot comprehend. He came from more than a parent; he came from complete unity with God his Father. Then he arrived on this planet, became flesh and dwelt among us.

> The Word became flesh and made his dwelling among us. We have seen his glory, the glory of the One and Only, who came from the Father, full of grace and truth. (John 1:14)

Any given night when you turn on the evening news, you will hear stories of war, poverty, hatred, murder, rape, abandonment and all types of evil. It was to this same kind of world that Jesus arrived.

As a mother and grandmother, I can't imagine a story line that would involve casting a beloved child into an uncaring place where he would be unaccepted, mistreated and finally murdered. But God did this out of his boundless love for us, knowing that Jesus was our only hope.

While God chose loving, spiritual parents to raise Jesus during his earthly childhood, this could not erase the separation from heaven that Jesus experienced. I imagine, since we are created in his image, that the Father felt indescribable pain as he watched his son suffer. Jesus certainly suffered, and Mary, Jesus' mother, learned early on that she would endure great pain. The prophet Simeon, upon meeting Mary with her new son, prophesied that a sword would pierce her very soul (Luke 2:35). What a riveting description of pain and loss!

Have you ever felt like a sword has pierced your soul?

Even with wonderful parents, Jesus was never fully "at home" here (Luke 2:49). Can you imagine the contrast of heaven and earth he must have felt? Jesus left perfection and incomprehensible beauty and relationship to begin his life on earth. When he was born, the first scent he smelled was warm animal dung; the first sounds he heard were the bleating cries of goats, instead of the rich melody sung by choirs of angels. As he grew up, Jesus' surroundings were unfamiliar and unknown.

Jesus provides healing when we feel we don't belong.

Do you ever ask yourself where you fit in or where you belong?

The person of Jesus not only shows us the way to that place that finally feels like home, but he longs to personally and tenderly carry us there. "There" is a place where we can feel at home within our own skin; where we can be at peace in our heart of hearts and where the "home fire" burns warmly inside of us. Jesus embodies the fulfillment for each and all of these longings with a place we can truly belong. He is our Wonderful Counselor, our Mighty God, our Everlasting Father and our Prince of Peace:

> For to us a child is born,
>   to us a son is given,
>   and the government will be on his shoulders.
> And he will be called
>   Wonderful Counselor, Mighty God,
>   Everlasting Father, Prince of Peace. (Isaiah 9:6)

As the mighty, understanding and limitless Lord, he is the healer for our primal wound:

> He heals the brokenhearted
>   and binds up their wounds.
> He determines the number of the stars
>   and calls them each by name.
> Great is our Lord and mighty in power;
>   his understanding has no limit. (Psalm 147:3–5)

Jesus has the credentials.

His experiences, combined with his love and power, provide the "connection point" for our own healing. Jesus is strong enough, deep enough, divine enough, human enough and complete enough to meet our needs no matter what we have experienced. He is our creator and sustainer, our Alpha and Omega. His ability to relate to us, combined with his reassuring love, offers us hope in a power and compassion that is greater than anything we have ever known or experienced.

As you approach each of these topics, you may find it is hard work to look at each of these issues with an intimate and personal application. You may realize you have not wanted to "go there," or you still have unresolved feelings, or you need to forgive someone. Thankfully, because of Jesus, you don't have to do this alone!

Perhaps most amazing is the fact that along with Jesus' understanding and power to meet our needs, he also has the desire to do so. He cares and wants to be involved with us every day. He wants to see us complete and fulfilled and to be part of His family as our perfect parent!

> Praise be to the God and Father of our Lord Jesus Christ, who has blessed us in the heavenly realms with every spiritual blessing in Christ. *For he chose us in him before the creation of the world to be holy and blameless in his sight. In love he predestined us to be adopted as his sons through Jesus Christ, in accordance with his pleasure and will— to the praise of his glorious grace, which he has freely given us in the One he loves.* In him we have redemption through his blood, the forgiveness of sins, in accordance with the riches of God's grace that he lavished on us with all wisdom and understanding. And he made known to us the mystery of his will according to his good pleasure, which he purposed in Christ... (Ephesians 1:3–9, emphasis added)

If you have experienced family disruption or other losses, you may experience life from a perspective that can be difficult to describe. It is as if no one else really understands your emptiness and longing for some elusive feeling of home. Natural history has been interrupted. You feel no "homeland security." The result is a soul filled with unrest and abandonment. There is a way to find rest for your soul. *In the presence of Jesus, this primal wound can find salve and healing deep inside your heart.*

> "Come to me, all you who are weary and burdened, and I will give you rest. Take my yoke upon you and learn from me, for I am gentle and humble in heart, and you will find rest for your souls. For my yoke is easy and my burden is light." (Matthew 11:28–30)

He can heal you because he has the limitless resources as the *son of God*. As the *son of man,* he has experienced what we feel. He understands Goose!

It is freeing to know that no matter where or to whom we were born, we all ultimately trace back to our Creator. Once we discover who we really are we can flourish. Once we discover "whose" we are we can no longer feel alone. We can finally "belong."

My prayer is that the messages in the following chapters will work their way into your heart and bring you hope as you come to know Jesus in a deeper way.

"When you come to the edge of all the light you know and are about to step into the darkness of the unknown, faith knows that one of two things will happen. There will be solid ground to stand on or you will be taught to fly."

– Author unknown

Jesus Completes Me
Jesus and Loss

2

According to Dr. Konrad Lorenz, Nobel Prize laureate and author of *The Year of the Greylag Goose,* geese possess a nearly human capacity for grief. Lorenz would frequently say, "Animals are much less intelligent than you are inclined to think, but in their feelings and emotions they are far less different from us than you assume." Quite literally, when they are grieving, a man, a dog and a goose will all hang their heads, lose their appetites, and become indifferent to all stimuli.[1]

For grief-stricken human beings, as well as for geese, one effect is that they become outstandingly vulnerable to accidents: they tend to fly into high-tension cables or fall prey to predators because of their reduced alertness. After the death of his beloved mate, a goose named Ado attached himself to Dr. Lorenz. According to Dr. Lorenz, "Ado would shyly creep up after me, his body hunched in sadness, and he would remain motionless about 25 or 30 feet away." Ado spent the remainder of the year sad and isolated.[2]

---

1. Dr. Konrad Lorenz, *The Year of the Greylag Goose,* (NY, NY: Harcourt Brace Jovanovich, Inc, 1979), pp. 31, 39.
2. *Love Canada Geese* website; "Do Canada Geese Mate for Life?", article by Choo Choo Love, Septemeber 21, 2006, http://www.articles.love-canadageese.com/lifemates.html.

Sobbing, Anna closed the door to what would have been her nursery. Her arms, eager to hold her baby, felt horribly empty after yet another miscarriage.

Joan started to dial the phone as she had done every day for years. She couldn't wait to share the news of her new job with her mom. Suddenly she threw the phone to the floor. No one was going to answer. Her mom had died and was no longer there to receive her call.

What losses have you experienced?

Think of things you have lost. Whether you are an adopted child, an adoptive parent or a child or spouse of divorce, you have experienced great loss. If you have lived through neglect or abuse, you know the pain of loss. If you have experienced the death of a family member or loved one, you understand that empty place in your heart. If you have dreamed to be married but are still single, or longed to have a child but are still childless, you know loss. Natural disasters and wars can bring devastating losses. If you have physical, emotional or even financial challenges, you have suffered loss. Losing a job, missing friends who have moved away, or watching your kids move out of the house may seem insignificant in comparison to the intense situations I have mentioned, yet they can produce many of the same feelings. Words on a page simply cannot do justice to the fear and emptiness these experiences bring.

My son Jacob lost contact with everything he had known. His native tongue and familiar sights and sounds were left across the ocean. He can never diagram a family tree. It has no known leaves. Perhaps, like Jacob, a move

28

has left you without your culture and your friends. Maybe you have lost touch with what should be basic for everyone—the nurturing from the one in whose womb you grew for 9 months. As an adoptive mom, I deeply love my son and strive to freely give him the love only a mother can know. Yet I believe that deep down he feels and grieves these losses in ways he does not know how to express.

How do we try to fill our sense of loss?

Losses leave an exaggerated emptiness in their wake; a void where you may find it difficult to be still and "at home with yourself." It is normal and necessary to grieve losses. Sometimes we don't understand the emotion that comes with loss and that we need to take the painful time needed to grieve. You may be familiar with recognized stages of grief: shock and denial, bargaining, anger, depression/sadness and lastly understanding/acceptance.[3]

Grief does not usually proceed through these stages in an orderly fashion, nor is it the same for each person. A loss that is grieved is like a wound that has left a scar—we do not feel sharp pain forever, and yet the reminder is never completely gone, either. Each new loss can bring forward unresolved feelings dating from earlier losses. We need to grieve our losses, yet it is often difficult to confront the loss and pain directly.

There are unhealthy things that happen when we stay alone in our sorrow and are thus left with a void. This emptiness often evokes in us restlessness or a wandering spirit that expresses itself in various ways:

You may go from relationship to relationship or job to job. You may try to fill losses with things that mask the pain whether it be alcohol, drugs, sex, pornography or even food.

---

3. See Appendix A.

You may keep yourself so busy there is little time to stop and feel emotions. You may strive for numerous accomplishments while trying to find that secure feeling you desire.

You may become preoccupied, anxious, or depressed, or you may just close off your feelings. You also might avoid getting close or vulnerable with others out of fear of future loss.

Perhaps you find you always desire to be in control, or that you obsess over neatness and order, or struggle with overpowering anger as you face this emptiness.

Intense losses often result in responses that may not necessarily fit with the situation at hand, yet they make sense to the one who feels the loss. A place, a smell or a particular action can inadvertently transport us back to the time of our deepest hurt. Years ago I had a dear friend whom I was training for the ministry, and so we spent a lot of time together. She was very effective at helping women learn the Bible and apply it to their lives.

During this time my husband and I decided we needed to take on a different ministry role that required a move to another state. She responded to this news negatively and became angry with me and isolated herself. Being young and inexperienced, I could not understand her actions. Later I came to discover something she hadn't disclosed to me at the time. As a trusting five-year-old girl, she went walking with her mother one day when they stopped at a crosswalk. Her mother told her to wait at that particular spot and then walked away. She kept walking and walking and never returned. She left her daughter on the corner. My friend had been abandoned. My heart ached as I learned this, and her actions then made complete sense to me. I had become the "mom figure," and in her mind a deep loss was being reenacted.

I remember well the first day I dropped Jacob off at school after he moved to the States to become part of our family. He was quite anxious, as he truly did not know if I would ever return for him. I made sure I was on time to

pick him up, as any tardiness on my part produced great fear inside of him. I can't imagine the fear he felt, but I understand that it was real for him.

When my father and then mother passed away, the loss I felt caused me to want to make decisions that made little sense at the time. In my childhood years I had grown up in a house with a pond in the backyard (where Gator Goose lived). Suddenly I had a strong desire to sell our home and find a house with a pond in the back. I held off, but the desire felt intense.

I have known others who, after experiencing loss, had a seemingly insatiable desire to be reassured of their own value. No matter how much love and assurance people gave them, it never felt like enough. There were still "holes" left in the soul.

Many people who feel this way don't want to go back to explore the source of these feelings. It seems too painful, and so they are tempted to ignore the causes and bury the wounds. However, unresolved core issues always find their way out in our thoughts and actions. In their wake we become more and more disconnected and unresolved.

One moment you feel that if you don't talk about what is inside you will explode, while the next moment you may feel it's too hard and complicated to open up—the words just won't come.

So how can Jesus relate? Did he feel loss? Can he fill loss?

Jesus experienced loss.

I cannot begin to imagine what it would be like to possess all power and wealth, to live in perfect love with no possibility of sickness or heartache, and then decide to leave it all for a world filled with sin, sickness, poverty and death. Jesus did this. Life in our world was unfamiliar to Jesus. Though we have never experienced a perfect world like Jesus did, we can share his experience of moving to unfamiliar territory.

Jesus took on a new form, new feelings, a new language, new sights, new smells and new parents. Not only did he experience the loss of everything he had known, but as he lived in this new form he continued to experience loss. As a toddler, he lost his first home when his parents had to flee to Egypt to escape Herod's terrifying pursuit of Jesus. Later on, at various times and to various degrees, Jesus lost his family's belief in him and support of him. He lost many friends, his good standing in Jewish society, and his comfort. On the cross, he lost his honor among the people. His name was mocked, and he even lost his clothes as they were auctioned. Finally, he lost his life. Jesus knows loss.

So what does Jesus have to do with my loss?

Since Jesus experienced loss, he can feel with us. He knows what it is like to feel great loss.

> For we do not have a high priest who is unable to sympathize with our weaknesses, but we have one who has been tempted in every way, just as we are—yet was without sin. (Hebrews 4:15)

Jesus can do more than sympathize; he also has the power to fill the void in our soul that comes from loss. Jesus gained new life through his resurrection! This resurrection enables him to be the author of life for us all by offering us a new and better life eternally—now. He came so that we might find life to the full (John 10:10).

> He was in the world, and though the world was made through him, the world did not recognize him. He came to that which was his own, but his own did not receive him. Yet to all who received him, to those who believed in his name, he gave the right to become children of God—children born not of natural descent, nor of human decision or a husband's will, but born of God. (John 1:10–13)

This scripture tells me that Jesus not only gives me the right but also the power to have a new life with a new birth. It also tells me I can be a true child of the creator of the universe. God knows that without this promise we will continue to have a lonely place in our soul. He has set a desire for "true home" in all of our hearts, because God is our true father and gives us a spiritual family and home.

> He has made everything beautiful in its time. He has also set eternity in the hearts of men; yet they cannot fathom what God has done from beginning to end. (Ecclesiastes 3:11)

How does Jesus fill up the emptiness our losses leave?

Jesus offers to make his home in us through His Spirit. A relationship with Jesus is the way to a new life and a new home that fills us that so we don't have to stay lonely despite our circumstances. He is the "bread of life;" the "resurrection and life;" the "light of the world;" the "gate for the sheep;" the "true vine;" the "living water;" the "good shepherd;" and "the way, the truth and the life." (John 6:35; 11:25; 8:12; 10:7; 15:1; 4:10; 7:38; 10:11,14; 14:6)

These descriptions tell me that:

As the bread of life, he fills up that empty feeling.

> Then Jesus declared, "I am the bread of life. He who comes to me will never go hungry, and he who believes in me will never be thirsty." (John 6:35)

I was moved to tears as I listened to Maria, Jacob's elderly friend from Romania, give accounts of the children reaching their frail arms through the orphanage gate as she handed them home-baked bread. Physically, the bread gave them relief from their hunger. The bread Jesus gives us tames the pain and gives rest to our souls. When Jesus through his spirit comes into our hearts to reside there (Acts 2:38), we find rest for our souls so our "eternal cells" gain strength.

As the resurrection and life, he makes us eternal beings.

> Jesus said to her, "I am the resurrection and the life. He who believes in me will live, even though he dies; and whoever lives and believes in me will never die. Do you believe this?" (John 11:25–26)

When we are born of God (Romans 6:3–6) we become new people filled with the same power that raised Jesus from the dead. We can possess eternal life spiritually, and never have to fear death.

> Therefore, if anyone is in Christ, he is a new creation; the old has gone, the new has come! (2 Corinthians 5:17)

This scripture tells us that the past is gone in God's eyes; we are wholly and completely forgiven of our sins. He gives us the power to change. Jesus is life, and allows us to have a fresh start to life.

As the light, he gives us direction.

> When Jesus spoke again to the people, he said, "I am the light of the world. Whoever follows me will never walk in darkness, but will have the light of life." (John 8:12)

Jesus, through his word and his presence, turns the light on in our lives so we can see him and walk in his steps. We don't have to walk in darkness any more, stumbling step by step.

Imagine walking in complete darkness, unsure of your next step. Sometimes that is the way losses make us feel. And yet imagine if, while we were still bumping into things, someone were to turn on the light, take our hand and guide us forward. What a relief! That's what Jesus does for us. He turns the light on.

As the light, Jesus also brings love, tenderness, compassion and relationships into our lives. Living in the shelter of his arms provides much needed warmth, which also results from light.

As the gate for the sheep, he lets us into his presence.

> "I am the gate; whoever enters through me will be saved. He will come in and go out, and find pasture." (John 10:9)

Jesus opens the door for us, allowing us to come into the very presence of God where we can find peace and contentment. He gives us all we need for proper boundaries and security through his word and his presence. The gate closed behind us assures us of spiritual safety. The gate opened in front of us assures us of our welcome. We can walk through this gate and finally be "home."

As the good shepherd, he protects us and knows us.

> "I am the good shepherd. The good shepherd lays down his life for the sheep...
>
> I am the good shepherd; I know my sheep and my sheep know me." (John 10:11,14)

> He tends his flock like a shepherd:
>   He gathers the lambs in his arms
> and carries them close to his heart;
>   he gently leads those that have young.
> (Isaiah 40:11)

Jesus urges us on and also corrects us with his "rod." He will lead us to quiet waters where we can be at peace in our souls. As our shepherd, he knows us by name and knows us intimately. Jesus is trustworthy, and as we follow him he leads us and stays with us even if we walk through the "shadow of death" (Psalm 23). He will come looking for us when we get lost and carry us in his arms when we are too tired to go on.

As the true vine, he is our connection to life and growth.

> "I am the true vine, and my Father is the gardener." (John 15:1)

> "I am the vine; you are the branches. If a man remains in me and I in him, he will bear much fruit; apart from me you can do nothing." (John 15:5)

As long as we stay connected to him, he will keep us nourished and help us grow. This connection gives life to our souls so we can bloom and have something to give to others.

As the living water, he is our refreshment and sustenance.

> "...but whoever drinks the water I give him will never thirst. Indeed, the water I give him will become in him a spring of water welling up to eternal life." (John 4:14)

He is the way we can start each day new and persevere day after day. We hear from him in his word and we talk to him in prayer. We can follow in his footsteps and have a real relationship with him. Our lives will be full to the point of overflowing from his promises. When we drink from him, our thirsts are truly quenched and our souls refreshed.

As the way, truth and life, he takes us directly to God.

> "Do not let your hearts be troubled. Trust in God; trust also in me. In my Father's house are many rooms; if it were not so, I would have told you. I am going there to prepare a place for you. And if I go and prepare a place for you, I will come back and take you to be with me that you also may be where I am. You know the way to the place where I am going."
>
> Thomas said to him, "Lord, we don't know where you are going, so how can we know the way?"
>
> Jesus answered, *"I am the way and the truth and the life.* No one comes to the Father except through me. If you really knew me, you would know my Father as well. From now on, you do know him and have seen him." (John 14:1–7, emphasis added)

Jesus and his words are complete truth; they don't change day to day. In this fact we can be secure and know that he is the one true constant in our lives. He will never change, nor will he leave us. He gives us the solid confidence and assurance that we can trust him. He always tells the truth, because he is *the* truth; we need look no further.

As one who will be with us always, he can be trusted.

> Then Jesus came to them and said, "All authority in heaven and on earth has been given to me. Therefore go and make disciples of all nations, baptizing them in the name of the Father and of the Son and of the Holy Spirit, and teaching them

to obey everything I have commanded you. *And surely I am with you always, to the very end of the age.*" (Matthew 28:18–20, emphasis added)

We can finally count on someone to never leave us or walk out on us. When we are alone and it feels like everyone else has gone, Jesus remains with us. We can walk away or send him away, but we would have to be the ones to walk. He will always be waiting for our return. This should bring us great security.

Jesus knows loss, feels our losses, and can fill the empty places in our hearts. Will you let him fill yours?

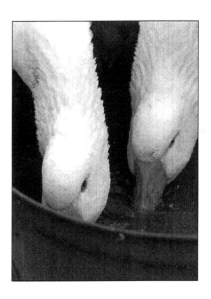

Jesus Chooses Me
Jesus and Rejection

3

> When I first met Gator Goose, he was alone...it
> seemed as if he were estranged from the other geese
> and ducks that frequented the pond in the back yard.
> I wasn't sure whether he was afraid to join the other
> geese, or if they did not accept him.

Elsie walked into her new classroom and felt eyes staring at her. She heard the giggles and whispers from a couple of kids sitting a few rows behind her. At the lunch table she pretended that she enjoyed eating alone, but could scarcely keep the welled-up tears from rolling down her cheeks. She didn't look like the other children and knew she wouldn't be included as their friend.

The alarm sounded, but Gabriella slammed it off. She didn't want to get up now or ever. Her pillow, wet from tears, supported her pounding head. Things still seemed surreal. Her marriage of twenty-two years was over. Her husband had informed her that he had never really loved her and was seeing someone else.

Daniel closed the door behind him in the orphanage. Prospective parents had been visiting and he had met them. His heart was beating through his chest. The visit was over, and he waited for days, weeks, months. He never heard from them again.

Have you ever been or felt rejected?

Rejection stings bitterly! It is a painful thing to be the object of prejudice, overlooked for a promotion, broken up with in a relationship, or even missing the cut on a team. These things hurt and can make us doubt ourselves or become angry and bitter. We can all remember details of specific situations where we experienced rejection, even as children. Words we hear can shout "rejection" to our ears. Have your heard any of the following?

I don't love you anymore...

I found someone else...

You weren't who we were looking for...

We no longer need your services...

You'll never amount to anything...

I wish you'd never been born...

A silence that loudly proclaims, "I don't care; you aren't worth caring about!"

You are such a disappointment...

Abandonment from family is perhaps the deepest of wounds. Disapproval, anger and criticism from parents have stayed with some adults their entire life.

My son grew up in a world without trust. He grew up in a country without trust. He was abandoned at birth. The one he should have been able to trust the most forsook him. Even though I tell him that we chose him (and we did!), Jacob knows that means his birth mother "unchose" him.

Think about some of the phrases people often say offhandedly: "You'd better be good or I'll put you up for adoption!"; or when people admire a newborn, they sometimes joke, "He's a keeper." All of these statements can imply to the adopted child who hears them, "I was not a keeper. I must be inherently bad because I was rejected."

Adopted children, as well as children growing up with neglect, abandonment or abuse, can tend to feel different or inferior in comparison to others even when great effort is made to help them feel accepted and loved.

Breakups, job terminations, disparaging looks and cutting words can also bring about feelings of rejection and worthlessness. We experience rejection and often assume we are to blame. How many spouses have assumed something was wrong with them because their partner has not deeply loved them? Parents who are absent emotionally or physically can often make their children think that they are not worth their time. Often, when we don't get a response we desire from another, we assume we are not smart enough, pretty enough or strong enough.

Birthday celebrations and holidays, while supposed to be fun and give honor, can often be unsettling to those who have experienced rejection. Birthdays are reminders of a day that should have turned out differently. Holiday gatherings can be reminders of what "might have been" were it not for rejection.

How do you respond to rejection?

With rejection, as with loss, comes the temptation to

close ourselves off to people or situations that might hurt us again.

Sometimes we may avoid encounters or conversations that call

Jesus Chooses Me

for vulnerability or openness. We may even try to sabotage a relationship. That way we can be the one who causes the relationship to fail before we have a chance to be rejected. This is a classic behavior for children in foster care.

We may become overachievers or people-pleasers, hoping to finally get the acceptance we long for.

When meeting rejection we may withdraw and harden our feelings, we might become aggressive, or we may become angry and bitter and blame others for our difficult situation. I have known many people who have faced harsh rejection of various kinds. One person will become angry and bitter, living a destructive lifestyle and hurting others in their wake. Another person with a very similar background will go on to live a life full of friendships and the desire to give and share with others.

The difference comes with our ability and willingness to forgive the past and to understand and believe that we are in fact valuable and valued!

If you have felt rejected, even rejected to the core of your being, take heart...

Jesus felt and understands rejection.

Jesus felt the deepest rejections possible. Throughout his life, Jesus' earthly family and friends were at times embarrassed of him. He was maligned and physically and verbally persecuted for his teachings. Some of his closest friends denied ever knowing him, thus allowing him to die on a cross. God himself ultimately had to reject Jesus in order to save us.

> And at the ninth hour Jesus cried out in a loud voice, "Eloi, Eloi, lama sabachthani?"—which

means, "My God, my God, why have you forsaken me?" (Mark 15:34)

Consider the words to the song "Call to Me" that express this so beautifully. The words are sung from God's perspective, speaking to his son.

Call To Me

It's time for you to go now, but I know you'll return,
Our love is there inside you, the children need to learn.
And though it won't be easy, you've got to be real strong,
And I will be here waiting, my son it won't be long.

Chorus:
Just call to me, and I will be right there,
When the weight of the world is heavy,
And there are no friends anywhere.

Just call to me and I will touch your heart
And the love will flow between us
Like it did right from the start

Well I know what you are thinking, but this was meant to be
You know we've never been apart for all of history
And the time will pass so slowly till we again are one
But you have got to show the world the Father and the Son

Chorus:
Just call to me, and I will be right there,
When the weight of the world is heavy,
And there are no friends anywhere.

Just call to me and I will touch your heart
And the love will flow between us
Like it did right from the start

The darkness will be there, confusing right from wrong,
To try and deceive you, kill your salvation song.

You will have to lie down, be nailed to a cross.
To save all our children. My son, that is the cost.

And when you call to me, I will not be there,
Pain will overtake you, the darkness will fill the air.
When you call to me, I must turn away.
There is no other way, no other way.

Death cannot keep a hold on you,
like the sun behind stormy skies,
I will take the stone away, and then you will rise
To show the people, that this was meant to be.
So we can be together, for all eternity.[1]

Jesus knows what it feels like to be rejected.

But how, other than sympathizing, can Jesus provide healing for our feelings of rejection?

Jesus accepts and loves me.

Jesus not only doesn't reject me...he unconditionally loves me. Jesus, God in the flesh, shows us this unconditional love of God that has been written about for many centuries. Reflect on the following scripture describing God's love for his people, Israel. No matter how unloved we may be or feel, Jesus wants us, Jesus chooses us.

> The word of the Lord came to me: "Son of man, confront Jerusalem with her detestable practices and say, 'This is what the Sovereign Lord says to Jerusalem: Your ancestry and birth were in the land of the Canaanites; your father was an Amorite and your mother a Hittite. On the day you were born your cord was not cut, nor were you washed with water to make you clean, nor were you rubbed

---

1. Words and music by Larry Jackson, used with permission.

with salt or wrapped in cloths. No one looked on you with pity or had compassion enough to do any of these things for you. Rather, you were thrown out into the open field, for on the day you were born you were despised.

"Then I passed by and saw you kicking about in your blood, and as you lay there in your blood I said to you, 'Live!' I made you grow like a plant of the field. You grew up and developed and became the most beautiful of jewels. Your breasts were formed and your hair grew, you who were naked and bare.

"Later I passed by, and when I looked at you and saw that you were old enough for love, I spread the corner of my garment over you and covered your nakedness. I gave you my solemn oath and entered into a covenant with you," declares the Sovereign Lord, "and you became mine.

"I bathed you with water and washed the blood from you and put ointments on you. I clothed you with an embroidered dress and put leather sandals on you. I dressed you in fine linen and covered you with costly garments. I adorned you with jewelry: I put bracelets on your arms and a necklace around your neck, and I put a ring on your nose, earrings on your ears and a beautiful crown on your head. So you were adorned with gold and silver; your clothes were of fine linen and costly fabric and embroidered cloth. Your food was fine flour, honey and olive oil. You became very beautiful and rose to be a queen. And your fame spread among the nations on account of your beauty, because the splendor I had given you made your beauty perfect," declares the Sovereign Lord. (Ezekiel 16:1–14)

Consider also Isaiah 49:15:

> "Can a mother forget the baby at her breast
> and have no compassion on the child she has
> borne?
> Though she may forget,
> I will not forget you!"

Jesus sees me for what I can be.

Jesus saw people in a way different than other people saw them. He sees us in this same way. Consider the Samaritan woman, the tax collector, the woman caught in adultery, the rich young ruler; even Judas. They were encumbered with sin, yet Jesus saw what they could become.

Jesus sees in us the beauty and purpose for which we were made. He sees beyond the surface to who we were created to be. He loves us unconditionally or he never would have come to earth. He did not look to see if we were good enough for him. He came anyway, he gave anyway. He loves anyway.

I can be secure in Jesus' love.

He never has and never will take back his love. He did not come to judge me but to save me.

If I hold on to him I can know that he will never let me go. He will never reject me as long as I hold on to him and his teachings.

> To the Jews who had believed him, Jesus said, "If you hold to my teaching, you are really my disciples. Then you will know the truth, and the truth will set you free." (John 8:31–32)

The poignant parable of the prodigal son (Luke 15:11-32) demonstrates that Jesus will never quit loving me even if I let go. He won't force me to stay. However, he will grieve if I run from him and yet await and hope for my return. His

hands are always there to hold me when I put mine in his. His hands will also guide and discipline me. (Discipline is an important component of love.) No matter what, however, the love does not go away. Human love fails, it is imperfect, but God's is different.

God's love never fails. It will continually fill us and keep us going.

> I took you from the ends of the earth,
>   from its farthest corners I called you.
> I said, 'You are my servant';
>   I have chosen you and have not rejected you.
> So do not fear, for I am with you;
>   do not be dismayed, for I am your God.
> I will strengthen you and help you;
>   I will uphold you with my righteous right hand.
> (Isaiah 41:9–10)

God chooses to make his home in my soul.

To remind me of his acceptance of me, God tells me that upon my spiritual birth he has given me his Spirit as proof that I am his (2 Corinthians 1:22; Ephesians 1:13), and has gone to prepare a place, a special room for me

(John.14:1-4). I will dwell with him forever in heaven, and until then he lives in the recesses of my soul; my heart of hearts. Even if all people reject me and misunderstand me for my background and their personal preferences, *Jesus wants me. He accepts me just as I am, not because I am so good. I never will be good enough and that's the point. He accepts me because He is so good.*

> "But I tell you the truth: It is for your good that I am going away. Unless I go away, the Counselor will not come to you; but if I go, I will send him to you." (John 16:7)

Can you imagine what it would be like to walk hand in hand with Jesus where he never leaves your side and you can ask for his advice on anything and everything? He told the disciples who spent every day with him that it would be *better* for him to go, so the Spirit could come be with them and live in them (John 16:6–8).

> To them God has chosen to make known among the Gentiles the glorious riches of this mystery, which is *Christ in you,* the hope of glory.
> We proclaim him, admonishing and teaching everyone with all wisdom, so that we may present everyone perfect in Christ. To this end I labor, struggling with all his energy, which so powerfully works in me. (Colossians 1:27–29, emphasis added)

> "If you love me, you will obey what I command. And I will ask the Father, and he will give you another Counselor to be with you forever—the Spirit of truth. The world cannot accept him, because it neither sees him nor knows him. *But you know*

him, for he lives with you and will be in you. I will not leave you as orphans; I will come to you. Before long, the world will not see me anymore, but you will see me. Because I live, you also will live. On that day you will realize that I am in my Father, and you are in me, and I am in you." (John 14:15–20, emphasis added)

Jesus Makes Me Innocent
Jesus on Shame and Guilt

4

While I was out on an afternoon walk last week, I noticed an injured goose lying on my neighbor's doorstep. A few yards away, its mate stood vigil. My neighbor, feeling nervous because of the protective stance of the mate, decided to call animal control to remove the goose. I felt sad for the hurt goose, but also for the other goose, who would not be able to protect its mate. The pair would not be able to withstand the "forces" that would eventually overcome them.

What do shame and guilt feel like for you?

Do you wish others didn't know your past, including that you were abused? Neglected? Divorced? Adopted? Not highly educated? Had an abortion? From alcoholic parents? From poverty? Had a less than righteous past? Do  you ever feel that if someone *really* knew everything about you they would not love you? You are not alone. Many people feel that their background makes

51

them inferior. They label themselves, just as if they had the word "Loser" pasted on their forehead. Their own actions can even become a self-fulfilling prophecy!

How do you respond to shame and guilt?

I remember well a conversation I had with Jacob when he failed the written driver's test the first time he took it. Understandably, the test was difficult for him to understand, with English as his new second language.

After the test he said, "I suck at life, I fail everything. Did your kids fail?"

I replied, "You are my kid."

To which he replied, "You know, your kids with blood."

One of my dear friends who grew up with abuse felt dirty and no good anymore. These feelings were so intense that she tried to cut and hurt herself on numerous occasions.

Children of divorce often struggle with feeling that their parents' separation is somehow their fault and are left with shame and guilt.

Scars from abortion leave shame and guilt.

Feelings of insecurity can run deep, and often find their roots in shame or guilt. We can feel guilty by our mere existence, sure that we are unworthy to take up space and other people's time, convinced that we do not deserve to be loved or accepted. I am brought to tears every time I remember a birthday when Jacob smashed his cake on the driveway and slammed his senior picture on the street. The glass shattered into tiny pieces. Looking at this situation objectively, it is easy to see that the shame and guilt that he felt was misplaced and unfitting. However, when this is your view of yourself, logic doesn't really fix the feeling.

Can Jesus really understand? How can the perfect Son of God relate to shame and guilt?

Throughout Jesus' life he was laughed at and persecuted for his teachings. He endured the cross, hanging as a common criminal. He had a crown of thorns placed on his head in mockery for being "King of the Jews." The cross was meant to inflict not just death, but a shameful death. To be placed on a cross was the ultimate social, physical, political and moral shame. It was used to tell the world that you were scum of the earth. You were exposed—naked and beaten and unable to breathe. One who was hanged on a cross became the object of scorn, ridicule and spit. Jesus' clothes were auctioned off and his life was mocked. Jesus became intimately acquainted with shame on the cross.

You may wonder how a person who has not sinned can relate to feelings of guilt. We can understand why guilt is placed on people who are sentenced for heinous crimes. Consider a serial killer's and rapist's sins, a child molester's sins, Hitler's sins, Pol Pot's and Ceausescu's sins. The devastating consequences from these people's wrongdoings are unthinkable, yet real. Jesus carried these sins, along with all of my sins, and your sins, on the cross. He even carried our "little" lies, our immorality, our selfishness and our greed to the cross. Thus, his father could have nothing to do with him as Jesus bore all of these at the cross. He took on that guilt and shame for us, for real. That is unimaginable and unthinkable, but it is true.

Jesus was familiar with shame and took on our guilt. The only way we can be relieved of this personal shame and guilt is by letting Jesus' blood and sacrifice pay for our sins (Romans 5:6–10). He knows how it feels, and yet he went way beyond empathy.

What causes our shame and guilt?

There are plenty of things we do that rightly cause us to feel shame and guilt. We have consciences, and they can either be tender toward God, or become hardened and seared. Our consciences are rightly disturbed when we don't live according to God's plan for us. As our creator, he knows what harms us and what is good for us. We don't have to wonder any more about what is right and what is wrong. Right and wrong is not determined by our feelings or even our consciences. God's word clarifies these things for us (Mark 7:20–23; Galatians 5:13–25). If we did not have real and deserved guilt, there would have been no reason for Jesus to come and pay the price our own sin requires.

However, we can also misplace shame and guilt for things that were done to us. *We need not feel guilt or shame for things that were done to us!* Too often, children who have been through painful things (like abuse, divorce, or adoption) don't understand that the situations they find themselves in *are not their fault*. We may not ever understand why we were put in a particular situation, yet we each must choose how we will respond to rejection and all painful experiences in our lives.

We can choose to listen to Jesus' view of us, or Satan's. In Revelation 12:10 we are told that Satan, the accuser, accuses us day and night. The voice we choose to listen to will determine many things in our future. Only God has the right to determine our value. Don't let others determine your value. Only Jesus can truly allow us to both feel and be free from guilt and shame.

Jesus can take away our shame and guilt.

The forgiveness Jesus offers us through his blood, which we share in at baptism (Romans 6:3–6), is big enough to completely take away our guilt.

That blood continually and completely keeps us clean and guilt-free as long as we are striving to follow him.

> This is the message we have heard from him and declare to you: God is light; in him there is no darkness at all. If we claim to have fellowship with him yet walk in the darkness, we lie and do not live by the truth. But if we walk in the light, as he is in the light, we have fellowship with one another, and the blood of Jesus, his Son, purifies us from all sin. (1 John 1:5–7)

Forgiveness and mercy are perhaps the most difficult gifts of Jesus to grasp and to accept. They seem too good to be true, too unreal and so undeserved. And therein is the meaning of mercy and forgiveness! They are undeserved, and yet we can be absolutely confident that Jesus gives them to us!

What does it mean to *be* forgiven? To *feel* forgiven? To *know* we're forgiven?

Each of us must understand and believe these truths about ourselves: Jesus can take away our sins in the waters of baptism (Acts 2:38). He has shown us that we are utterly valuable and that we are worth his entire life, because we were worth his death.

All we have to do is stick with him, following him in the light, walking with him side by side, and we will keep on being forgiven. We can then walk with confidence as a child of the King of Kings and Lord of Lords.

Jesus Knows Me
Jesus and Identity

5

Geese can "imprint" with humans or with other animals, causing them to think they are a species other than goose! Gator Goose's attachment to my parents caused him to think he was more human than goose.

Do you sometimes not know who you really are? Do you often have a hard time figuring out where you belong?

This is normal enough when we know our family and its history well. When we don't know our historical roots, our identity crisis is exaggerated.

As mentioned earlier, I recently lost both of my parents, whom I dearly loved. It was unsettling to not have the people around who gave me birth and knew me and loved me unconditionally. I felt orphaned, even though

I'd had a half century of knowing them and being loved by them! If this loss was so difficult for me to process, consider the added pain experienced by people "born outside of their family," people who have never known their biological roots. Their family trees have lost all their leaves. I don't say this to imply that adoptive parents are not real family. But many adoptees still feel a deep sense of lost identity for their whole lives, no matter how lovingly they are embraced by their adoptive families. People in blended families and broken families can share these same insecurities. We were once someone's spouse, someone's parent, someone's child—and then things changed. Even a change in our job can leave us unsure of who we are. We may be left with an identity crisis.

We all want to know and be known for who we are and whose we are.

Jacob's identity and even his ethnicity can be confusing. He has faced racial slurs. He has been stereotyped. Often people have said insensitive things like asking how he fit into our family since he looked different from the rest. Our identity is important to us. It can connect us, confuse us, or accuse us. Other people often are not helpful to us in confirming our identity.

I remember well an experience that exemplifies this dilemma. It had been less than a year since September 11, 2001. Jacob had been to our church teen camp and was riding home with one of the counselors and another teenager. Jacob and the other teen did not fit the "Caucasian male" stereotype. Jacob was asleep in the back seat when the counselor who was driving pulled off of an exit to find a restroom. As he turned off the exit, eight state patrol cars surrounded his car with guns pointed at them. The troopers told all three to come out of the car with their hands up. They frisked them and put them in separate cruisers and began to harshly question them.

As the plot unfolded, it seemed a trucker had passed the boys earlier and had spotted a pea shooter (a kind of toy gun) resting in the other boy's lap (the boys had used it during their camp games). Within a few moments, while minding their own business, these boys had become suspects for a robbery that had happened a few hours earlier in a nearby town. After much commotion, everything was straightened out and apologies were given to the boys. Jacob and his friend "looked suspicious," and their identity came under fire. (I've often thought that my son experienced a *My Cousin Vinny* scenario in real life!) How quickly assumptions of our identity can be made! These can have many consequences and affect us deeply.

In another situation, when my oldest granddaughter was born, she was immediately whisked down the hall in an incubator, past the watchful eyes of her exuberant and anxious extended family. On the other side of the hall, my daughter had just undergone an emergency C-section. She had awakened that morning excited to attend her baby shower. Instead, a few hours later baby Emma arrived on the scene, six weeks premature. The family crowded around the incubator in order to see this precious bundle as the nurses brought her through the waiting room. Our hearts were elated that she was healthy and that Melissa, her mom, was fine.

Baby Emma filled our hearts with love, yet we were all concerned about her health as a premature infant. Our celebration was filled with tears and laughter. Jacob stood off in the corner happy for "us." When I asked him to come over closer to see he said, "No, you can look. It's your family."

I knew that inherent in this statement was the oft-repeated feeling that he didn't really belong to the family.

When Jacob first came to our family, he would say his middle name was "Van Damme." He didn't like the middle name we gave him—Richard, in honor of my dad. He would never think of using it. However, when we are proud of who we are named for, our pride in our identity grows. When Richard, my dad, passed away several years ago, many wonderful things were shared about him at his funeral. His grandsons served as his pallbearers. After hearing these wonderful things shared about my dad and learning more of who he was, I noticed that Jacob signed the form he was asked to sign as a pallbearer as "Jacob *Richard* Shaw." It was now a name he wore proudly.

Perhaps if we would really get to know Jesus, we would fully understand the privilege of being called "Christian." What an identity!

When we are unsure of who we really are, how does it affect us?

Insecurity reigns when we are not confident of who we really are. Insecurity can cause us to withdraw from people, or it can cause us to be overly aggressive, trying to prove our worth. We can tend to feel threatened when a weakness we have is seen by someone else, which may make us come across as prideful. Simple suggestions we receive can cause us to shut down or to get angry at the messenger. Insecurity can tempt us to "drink" confidence in alcohol or pills.

Our confusion about our identity may result in a desire

to be accepted by others to a point where we become people-pleasers to the extreme. We desire to fit in and be accepted for who we think someone wants us to be, or we may
(without realizing it) look for relationships with people who
treat us badly, somehow thinking that is what we deserve.

Jesus can understand our feelings when we feel we don't really fit in.

Jesus grew up living with his parents, Mary and Joseph.
He was a carpenter's son. Yet at twelve years old, Jesus realized that there was somewhere he felt more "at home"
than when he was at home with his physical family. He
wandered away to be about his heavenly Father's business.
His family could not find him for several days, and when
they finally found him, we was sitting in the temple—God's
house: "Why were you searching for me?" he asked. "Didn't
you know I had to be in my Father's house?" (Luke 2:49)

How did Jesus possess such a sure sense of identity?

How did he live in this "adopted" family with a new
culture, a new language, and even a new way of measuring
time? How could he have such a strong understanding of
who he was, even as a young boy? How could he come to
know "true north," where he came from and where he was
going, even in early adulthood?

> Jesus answered, "Even if I testify on my own be-
> half, my testimony is valid, for I know where I
> came from and where I am going. But you have no
> idea where I come from or where I am going."
> (John 8:14)

What difference did Jesus' view of himself make in his handling of temptation and suffering, and in his responses to others' actions and views of him?

> Later they sent some of the Pharisees and Herodians to Jesus to catch him in his words. They came to him and said, "Teacher, we know you are a man of integrity. You aren't swayed by men, because you pay no attention to who they are; but you teach the way of God in accordance with the truth. Is it right to pay taxes to Caesar or not?" (Mark 12:13–14)

- He did not feel threatened.
- He was not a people-pleaser, trying to fit in.
- He did not feel inadequate or insecure.
- He kept on doing the will of God for his life (he learned obedience).
- He entrusted himself to God who judges justly.

> *Jesus knew that the Father had put all things under his power, and that he had come from God and was returning to God; so* he got up from the meal, took off his outer clothing, and wrapped a towel around his waist. After that, he poured water into a basin and began to wash his disciples' feet, drying them with the towel that was wrapped around him. (John 13:3–5, emphasis added)

- He did not feel unworthy due to upbringing, culture or education.
- He never felt servile while serving others; he simply focused on serving God.
- He had inner certitude, which made him impervious to criticism and rejection.

What does this have to do with me, you ask?

Ask yourself: What voices do I listen to and allow to affect my view of myself? What tapes play in my head over and over again?

Tell yourself: Jesus can be the source of my identity. I'm the child of the creator of the universe, King of Kings and Lord of Lords.

The empty place in our heart and our soul can be filled. But first we must know where we really come from and where we are going. Ultimately, we all trace back to the same source. Remember that the scriptures state in Ecclesiastes 3 that we are created by God with "eternity in our hearts."

He thought us up, formed us and made us come alive. We are fearfully and wonderfully made. We are not mistakes.

> For you created my inmost being;
>> you knit me together in my mother's womb.
> I praise you because I am fearfully and
>> wonderfully made;
>> your works are wonderful,
>> I know that full well.
> My frame was not hidden from you
>> when I was made in the secret place.
> When I was woven together in the depths of the
>> earth,
>> your eyes saw my unformed body.
> All the days ordained for me
>> were written in your book
>> before one of them came to be.
> (Psalm 139:13–16)

Then God said, "Let us make man in our image, in our likeness, and let them rule over the fish of the sea and the birds of the air, over the livestock, over all the earth, and over all the creatures that move along the ground."

So God created man in his own image,
in the image of God he created him;
male and female he created them.
(Genesis 1:26–27)

Jesus is God in the flesh. He was called Emmanuel, which means "God with us." When God's spirit dwells within us we are home. Having Jesus inside our heart and soul is the only way we can truly feel "at home in our own skin." Only then do we have the confidence to connect with others.

Jesus replied, "If anyone loves me, he will obey my teaching. My Father will love him, and we will come to him and *make our home with him.*" (John 14:23, emphasis added)

Jesus Is Trustworthy
Jesus on Intimacy and Trust

6

Several months ago in a Buffalo, New York, cemetery, a mother goose lost her lifelong mate and was left alone to tend her eggs. She had chosen an empty cemetery urn for her nest, and she spent the days sheltering her eggs from the cool spring air.

The loss of her male partner made her vulnerable to any would-be predators. However, in an unlikely twist of fate, an adult deer took over the role of protector. If passersby approached the area, the deer would place himself between the person and the nesting goose. On one occasion the deer even had a standoff with a barking dog!

There's no known way that a deer and goose can communicate, yet somehow the deer came to understand the nesting mother's need.

More than eight years ago, I became a grandmother. (Have I already mentioned this?) Now I have five wonderful grandchildren, which is an incredible privilege and blessing. It sobers and amazes me to watch the circle of life, now that I have many more years of life experience "under my belt." As I watch my grandchildren, I see more clearly how they develop security and trust at such young ages. The earliest years are described as "formative years" for a reason.

What makes it hard for you to trust?

As babies, children in nurturing homes learn that when they feel hungry, scared, sad, happy, or lonely, they will get an immediate response and reassurance. But children who are born into neglect and other types of abuse, children whose parents were absent physically or emotionally, and children born into extreme poverty and war—all begin their lives feeling the same needs, but their needs are rarely met. They find no reassurance, and so they do not build trust in their formative years. Emotions often become associated

 with pain...then apathy...then atrophy. Life often centers around survival, with trust for no one. Intimacy can be nonexistent. Can you relate personally to this experience, or have you seen this pattern in someone you know?

How do you respond to broken trust?

Many people struggle to trust because they've had legitimate reasons *not* to trust the people who should have been the most dependable, the most trustworthy. They fear being hurt again too much to risk becoming vulnerable. Is it hard for you to be vulnerable, to feel or express your needs, or to trust anyone?

So often we go back to our "default" places of mistrust and fear even when something or someone is trustworthy.

It is hard to trust when we look back at our pain instead of toward the one who is worthy of trust.

If you have difficulty moving forward in a relationship or moving on after a broken relationship, if you remember all the offenses done toward you, or if you have difficulty sharing your true feelings, it is unlikely you have decided to trust. Perhaps you are sure that someone in your life is untrustworthy. That may certainly be the case, but don't let it steal your trust for the One who is always worthy of trust.

> But I am like an olive tree
>   flourishing in the house of God;
> I trust in God's unfailing love
>   for ever and ever. (Psalm 52:8)

> When I am afraid,
>   I will trust in you.
> In God, whose word I praise,
>   in God I trust; I will not be afraid.
>   What can mortal man do to me? (Psalm 56:3–4)

> It is better to take refuge in the Lord
>   than to trust in man.
> It is better to take refuge in the Lord
>   than to trust in princes. (Psalm 118:8–9)

> Who among you fears the Lord
>   and obeys the word of his servant?

Let him who walks in the dark,
    who has no light,
trust in the name of the Lord
    and rely on his God. (Isaiah 50:10)

"Do not let your hearts be troubled. Trust in God; trust also in me." (John 14:1)

How can Jesus relate to our struggles with vulnerability and trust?

Jesus gave his heart to people and it got stepped on again and again. He knows the temptation to withhold his heart and not trust anyone. His friends left him; some even betrayed him. His closest friends could not even share with him the hurt he was feeling in the garden before his death. They fell asleep.

> Then Jesus went with his disciples to a place called Gethsemane, and he said to them, "Sit here while I go over there and pray." He took Peter and the two sons of Zebedee along with him, and he began to be sorrowful and troubled. Then he said to them, "My soul is overwhelmed with sorrow to the point of death. Stay here and keep watch with me."
> Going a little farther, he fell with his face to the ground and prayed, "My Father, if it is possible, may this cup be taken from me. Yet not as I will, but as you will."
> Then he returned to his disciples and found them sleeping. "Could you men not keep watch with me for one hour?" he asked Peter. (Matthew 26: 36–40)

Jesus' trust in God allowed him to be vulnerable and to trust. Our trust in God will allow us to be vulnerable and to trust.

Jesus still found a way to give his heart away again and again even after he was betrayed. While on the cross, looking at those who had mocked, tortured and betrayed him, he was able to find the words, "Father, forgive them, they do not know what they are doing" (Luke 23:34). He still keeps giving his heart to you and me every day. After he was resurrected, he chose to entrust his message and ministry to men and women, most of whom had recently denied him. This is who he is. He loves—and so he gives and keeps on giving. Why could he do this? Because he entrusted himself to the one who judges justly:

> To this you were called, because Christ suffered for you, leaving you an example, that you should follow in his steps.
>
> "He committed no sin,
> and no deceit was found in his mouth."
>
> When they hurled their insults at him, he did not retaliate; when he suffered, he made no threats. Instead, he entrusted himself to him who judges justly. (1 Peter 2:21–23)

He entrusts his entire message of reconciliation to us (2 Corinthians 5:14–20). He never quit trusting God. His heart was with God first and foremost, and that enabled him to keep on giving. People will let us down. We will let people down. Yet God remains faithful:

> ...If we are faithless, he will remain faithful, for he cannot disown himself. (2 Timothy 2:13)

God's plan was for children to be loved and to be taught security, love, and the basics of life. When they are not, God is grieved. God is not the one to blame.

> What if some did not have faith? Will their lack of faith nullify God's faithfulness? Not at all! *Let God be true, and every man a liar.* (Romans 3:3–4, emphasis added)

Our free choice allows each of us to choose the way we will live, either ignoring God's plan or following his plan. When we don't follow God's plan, we remain empty and have little to give. We then keep on getting hurt and hurting others.

At some point we must realize that trust is a decision.

We will never reach a point where all the stars align for us and no one ever hurts us or disappoints us again. When we put our trust in the One who is bigger than us (and everyone else!), we can then gain confidence and security to reach out to others again and again...because God's love is deep enough, wide enough and high enough to continually fill us.

It is impossible to give love when we don't feel loved or secure. We become too busy trying to fill up our own life—an impossible task without Jesus.

All the stuff in the world (the money, toys, gadgets, relationships, alcohol, vacations, drugs and accomplishments) won't take away our deep and inherent need for trust, intimacy and security. This need that can only be filled by God.

> Jesus is the same yesterday, today and forever. (Hebrews 13:8)

He is worthy of all trust. He does not run out of love for us. When we grasp the height, depth and width of God's love, we can become a giver because we are then filled from within and have something to give.

> And I pray that you, being rooted and established in love, may have power, together with all the saints, to grasp how wide and long and high and deep is the love of Christ, and to know this love that surpasses knowledge—that you may be filled to the measure of all the fullness of God. (Ephesians 3:17b–19)

When we can feel loved, we can then give love. When we give love, it results in deep joy.

Jesus Can Take the Wheel
Jesus and Control

7

No matter how much he hissed and fussed while "protecting" my parents from the mailman or the friends who came to visit them, Gator Goose could not control the outcome of their lives—or of his own life.

Do you feel uncomfortable when you are not in control of your life? Does being out of control make you feel vulnerable? Do you hate to "mess up" and see imperfections in your life? Does the following statement ring true for you:

When I'm not able to be open with my thoughts, fears and weaknesses, I take control; when I don't trust, I'm anxious.

Why do you try to take control of the settings and situations around you?

While none of us have any control over how we came into this world, some people were dealt a more painful hand than others. Adopted children; children who have lost a parent or parents; children from broken homes; and children with alcoholic, abusive or neglectful parents can feel more intensely the life-changing choices that were made for them. These choices involved them deeply, and yet they had no say in them. They could not even control their most basic of needs—being cared for and feeling safe with those who should have protected them.

Often when our situation in life is confusing and unfair, our desire to be in control increases. Perhaps we think if we stay in control we can avoid more pain.

How does "taking control" show itself in daily life?

My friend "Sarah" grew up with an alcoholic parent. She can seem obsessive over cleanliness in her home. If things are messed up or out of place, she tends to feel a sense of panic. At times her husband and children feel she is like a helicopter, hovering above them, trying to control the details of the comings and goings of their daily lives.

From the beginning of his life, my son Jacob had little control over his life. He did not choose to be abandoned. He did not choose where he would live, and when he lived in the orphanage, he could not choose what he would eat or even when he could use the bathroom facility. As he grew to be an older child, he did not choose his schedules and routine in the orphanage. Those were chosen for him.

I believe something strongly within him says, "I will not feel loss again; I will not feel the pain of rejection. I will not feel or get close…I will just survive." Do you feel this way? The cardinal rule of survival is: Keep yourself in control by any and all means, since no one else can be trusted. No distractions (like feelings) are allowed to get in the way.

To feel need is the opposite of being a survivor. Survivors learn to fend for themselves. Previous experience has taught them that no one will be there for them, and so they often create an insulated way of life. They won't often rely on anyone else. This breeds a lonely and defensive way of living, and creates an internal resistance to trusting relationships.

Unfortunately this goes against the premise of Christianity. Finding a relationship with God stems from the realization that we *need* God. It's good and right to feel need. Though we desperately need relationships with God and others, the desire to control often blocks our ability to build real, meaningful relationships. These relationships are where we know and express our need for God and people and allow ourselves to trust.

People with a survivor mentality feel they must stay in control. They get into the habit of always scrutinizing the situation around them and figuring out the "system." Survivors try to figure out the system surrounding them in order to make or manipulate it to work for them. Many survivors, especially those who have experienced a great deal of trauma, may find that their eyes are always literally (and involuntarily) looking from side to side, a protective instinct.

Freedom is a big deal to all of us, yet the desire to be free and answer to no one is often exaggerated by those who feel they have had less control than others. Sadly, early on Jacob had no one in his life who truly cared for him. It was very hard for him to suddenly have parents in his life who did care and to whom he was accountable. Once when I asked him what he would like for me as a parent to change, his response was simply, "You care too much. I don't want you to care." Part of this, I believe, stemmed from the fact that deep down he didn't believe he was worth caring about.

Love complicates our survival mechanism.

When we start caring, we feel responsibility toward others, as well as the need for trust to be given and built.

Jesus can relate to our feelings of wanting to be in control

Jesus certainly was tempted (even during his first recorded temptation in the desert) with taking control. He was all-powerful and could have controlled his own destiny to go down a different path. He didn't have to hurt over his friends. He didn't have to lose sleep, to care, or to love. He didn't have to go to the cross. He didn't have to die.

Jesus was perhaps most tempted to take control prior to the cross—the event that would change history and allow us all a chance to change. He asked his disciples to watch and pray with him, and he prayed so intensely that his sweat was like drops of blood as he tried to surrender his will to God's:

> Jesus went out as usual to the Mount of Olives, and his disciples followed him. On reaching the place, he said to them, "Pray that you will not fall into temptation." He withdrew about a stone's throw beyond them, knelt down and prayed, "Father, if you are willing, take this cup from me; yet not my will, but yours be done." An angel from heaven appeared to him and strengthened him. And being in anguish, he prayed more earnestly, and his sweat was like drops of blood falling to the ground.
>
> When he rose from prayer and went back to the disciples, he found them asleep, exhausted from sorrow. "Why are you sleeping?" he asked them.

"Get up and pray so that you will not fall into temptation." (Luke 22:39–46)

Jesus chose to come here and chose to die here; and he did it for you and me. *He exchanged control for giving himself up.* He could have called ten thousand angels to take him off of the cross.

"Put your sword back in its place," Jesus said to him, "for all who draw the sword will die by the sword. Do you think I cannot call on my Father, and he will at once put at my disposal more than twelve legions of angels? But how then would the Scriptures be fulfilled that say it must happen in this way?" (Matthew 26:52–54)

Something or someone will control each of our lives. Seeing how Jesus handled himself in the garden shows me that I don't need to try and control every difficult situation I encounter.

Ask yourself: Is it really working when you are trying to take control? Is it producing security, intimacy, trust, sense of identity and purpose, fulfillment and freedom from guilt?

If not, then would it not be much safer and much smarter to let Jesus to take control of your life?

Imagine the thrill of being on a fast train, speeding through the countryside toward your destination. But what if this train begins to feel "too confined and controlled" from staying on the track for which it was designed? In an effort to take over the controls, to be truly free and see the world its own way, the train might decide to jump off the track in search of freedom. We can be like that train, wanting to "jump the track" and take the controls. The result is

always the same. It ends with a train wreck.

Meanwhile, when we allow Jesus to take control of us while we are on the track he has set out for our lives, we can learn what it means to really be free. We can drive at our full, intended speed and even learn to enjoy the scenery as we ride.

Making Progress

8

During the early summer days in New England, I enjoy watching the growth of the newly hatched fuzzy little goslings. I see them often as I pass by open fields and parking lots. Over the next couple of months they will face many challenges to their survival, but by the time they are three months old they will begin to soar!

Progress

Overcoming the issues we have discussed may seem overwhelming and nearly impossible. However, it's important to remember that while this is impossible by human standards, nothing is impossible with God.

God remembers what we have been through; God is always attentive and is always at work.

> Jesus said to them, "My Father is always at his work to this very day, and I, too, am working." (John 5:17)

And we also thank God continually because, when you received the word of God, which you heard from us, you accepted it not as the word of men, but as it actually is, the word of God, which is at work in you who believe. (1 Thessalonians 2:13)

When our first three children were young, our family used to sing a song entitled "Little by Little." I still repeat some of the words when I become impatient:

Little by little and day by day; little by little in every way my Jesus is changing me…

He's changing me, my precious Jesus, he's changing me day by day.

Sometimes it's slow going, but there's a knowing…that some day, perfect I will be.[1]

Waiting is hard. Meanwhile, I take comfort that my weaknesses can one day be strengths:

But he said to me, "My grace is sufficient for you, for my power is made perfect in weakness." Therefore I will boast all the more gladly about my weaknesses, so that Christ's power may rest on me. That is why, for Christ's sake, I delight in weaknesses, in insults, in hardships, in persecutions, in difficulties. For when I am weak, then I am strong. (2 Corinthians 9:10)

I also have hope in the fact that God's spirit changes me from one degree of glory to another.

Now the Lord is the Spirit, and where the Spirit of the Lord is, there is freedom. And we, who with

---

1. Song by Elsie Dietz Lippy.

unveiled faces all reflect the Lord's glory, are being transformed into his likeness with ever-increasing glory, which comes from the Lord, who is the Spirit. (2 Corinthians 3:17–18)

God answers my prayers, although often not on my time schedule or with *my* seemingly incredible ideas.

I have come to realize that the things I experience and feel are not really about someone else. They make up my personal journey. We all have journeys of our own. The choices we make in responding to our journeys are extremely important!

The converging paths of my journey and Jacob's journey have often been much harder than I could have ever imagined, and I have learned and I am learning so much from them. Across the miles there have been many detours that felt like huge boulders in the road. These have molded me, sobered me, taught me and refined me. The hardest  parts to travel have given me the opportunity to become a better person. Without them I certainly would have been a much less compassionate and much more judgmental person. I have come to understand Jesus so much more through the small trials I have faced.

This journey is one that only Jesus, full of grace and truth, could empower me to travel. I could not do it on my own. I had to come to grips with my own struggle with loss, identity, guilt, rejection, trust and control. I had to depend on Jesus.

I look back over the last couple of years and thank God for many prayers I see being answered. The progress in my relationship with Jacob has been astounding, in spite of the many times when I wondered if we would ever see any victories. So often I felt hopeless and struggled for faith. I am grateful, and so proud of Jacob for the ways he has worked to grow and to figure out life and make it work, "little by little and day by day…"

You have a choice.

Jesus offers you a choice. You can continue with a longing and emptiness in your soul, or be filled by him and become complete. No matter where life's road has taken you there is always a choice of how you will journey through it. Jesus can't make anyone love him or follow him, no matter how deeply he desires that relationship. From Jesus you can learn and find rest for your soul.

I have learned that I can't determine anyone else's path. All I can do is choose the way *I* will travel. On my journey, I have come to struggle with many of these core issues of loss and identity myself. Without Jesus, I would be without hope. With him, I am full of hope; I can break the shackles and begin to soar.

During a time that was particularly painful and bleak, I realized that even amidst and because of the pain, I was actually growing stronger and deeper in my relationship with God and other people. I was more desperate for God's words and touch, and I could empathize more keenly with others around me. I have come to realize, as the Scriptures promise, that some of the darkest hours are the ones that mold, shape and refine us the most. They are the ones that make us more useful to God and to those around us.

Be forewarned that if we do not become stronger and more giving through our trials, we will not only miss out on amazing opportunities to grow and give, but we will also tend towards becoming bitter and cynical in our attitude. This not only keeps us from God but also further alienates us from vital relationships and from the healing we so greatly need.

> See to it that no one misses the grace of God and that no bitter root grows up to cause trouble and defile many. (Hebrews 12:15)

> In this you greatly rejoice, though now for a little while you may have had to suffer grief in all kinds of trials. These have come so that your faith—of greater worth than gold, which perishes even though refined by fire—may be proved genuine and may result in praise, glory and honor when Jesus Christ is revealed. Though you have not seen him, you love him; and even though you do not

see him now, you believe in him and are filled with an inexpressible and glorious joy, for you are receiving the goal of your faith, the salvation of your souls. (1 Peter 1:6–9)

Disney's Dumbo the elephant says it well when he states, "The very things that held you down are going to carry you up." Don't let the difficulties you have suffered be wasted. As you find comfort, take the opportunity before you to encourage others and help them see God. It is through giving of ourselves that we will find joy restored to our souls.

Praise be to the God and Father of our Lord Jesus Christ, the Father of compassion and the God of all comfort, who comforts us in all our troubles, so that we can comfort those in any trouble with the comfort we ourselves have received from God. For just as the sufferings of Christ flow over into our lives, so also through Christ our comfort overflows. (2 Corinthians 1:3–5)

Personal Reflections

9

Writing this book has been a journey in itself! Through its pages, I have relived several difficult moments from my life. As I have thought through my own experiences, I have come to some unexpected realizations about how I have handled (and continue to handle) all of the feelings we've discussed:

Loss

I, too, have grieved. I grieve for the difficulty Jacob has had in feeling like he is truly my son because of the lost childhood years with us, and I grieve for all the losses I cannot restore in his life. There are so many things I cannot go back and repair because I was not able to be there for him in his formative years. I cannot change that fact.

I have grieved for lost parents and other family members, and for dear friends who have moved away. I have grieved because of moves and job changes that have altered my dreams.

I choose to respond by finding God and his way through these things, not by continually reacting to these hurts with thoughts and actions that derail me from God's plan. What will you choose?

Rejection

Many days, I have felt Jacob's total rejection of me. When I first began writing this several years ago, I wrote, "Every day I feel his rejection." But within the past several years, now that Jacob is living on his own, I have come to realize that I no longer feel his rejection at all. In fact, I have come to feel his love. I stand amazed at the progress in our relationship. I love spending time with him. That change has been so dramatic that I can scarcely believe what I am writing.

Shame and Guilt

Truthfully, I sometimes used to feel shame because of the way that Jacob "represented" his family to other people. But that was my problem. Thankfully, I have grown beyond that. Jacob is who he is, and I love him unconditionally. I am very proud of him and I pray that he will feel the same way toward himself. I have also felt guilt for not being able to reach him at times—feeling that I had failed, wondering what else I might have done. I have also felt guilty when I have responded with anxiety and fear. I have sometimes been tempted to give up and lose confidence. I've had to decide to rely on the convictions and relationships I have come to know from God. Who will you rely on?

Identity

During some of the toughest times I began to wonder if I was a bit crazy. I would wonder, "Who am I but 'trash' to this son that I love?" I became the target of much of the baggage he carried with him, as well as a target of his ma- nipulation. I had to learn to set proper boundaries of responsibility, and to refocus my self-image on who God tells me I am. I had to learn that I could decide how I would live life and not let someone else steal my God-given identity. Who will you allow to determine your identity?

Intimacy and Trust

How I have longed to have Jacob tell me what he was feeling inside and to have true closeness with him! I have longed for him to feel safe enough to need my love—but most importantly, God's love. I want for him to really know me and for me to know him. This is a growing process. I have had to renew my decision each day to trust God with this relationship. I have also had to guard against allowing anxiety over Jacob to hamper my intimacy in other relationships.

I longed to trust Jacob when I couldn't, yet now he has continued to grow more trustworthy. This process has taken many years, and yet I am so encouraged by the mutual trust I now share with Jacob. Will you decide to trust God with your relationships?

Control

How I have battled the desire to take control! I couldn't control Jacob, so I finally learned that I might as well stop trying to "police" him. The great challenge was to not let his choices control me and my peace; I found that quite difficult much of the time. Only in daily prayer and encouragement from others could I find peace. I had to accept in my heart that what someone else does is their choice and their life. I can offer love and provide helpful opportunities...but I can't make their decisions. What a journey of growth that has been for me.

I can only navigate my journey successfully through Jesus' example and presence in my life. I go back to the scripture where I began,

> "Come to me, all you who are weary and bur-
> dened, and I will give you rest. Take my yoke upon
> you and learn from me, for I am gentle and humble
> in heart, and you will find rest for your souls. For
> my yoke is easy and my burden is light."
> (Matthew 11:28–30)

I thank Jacob for all the lessons he has taught me. I love him deeply and am grateful for my son. I see more clearly than ever the loving and caring young man that he is. I see him fight through things that are very hard. I see him wanting to grow and be successful, and wanting his life to have meaning. I see him wanting to help others and continually finding ways to do so. Part of this is the progress I have made in how I view him, but so much is the progress Jacob has made. As we both keep on growing, I only look forward to seeing where this journey takes us. I'm grateful we are both still walking it and grateful we are walking much closer together than we ever have before.

Finding Your Place to Belong

10

As I began this book with the story of a goose, I want to close speaking about our feathered friends.

Geese are fascinating birds. I love springtime around my house, where I may occasionally stop to let a goose mother and father, along with their little goslings, cross the road. A number of years ago I had a camera in the car and snapped this picture of a little goose family crossing a busy intersection in my town.

God intends for each of us to be in a family. The church that Jesus established is God's family.

God puts us in a family.

> His intent was that now, through the church, the manifold wisdom of God should be made known to the rulers and authorities in the heavenly realms, according to his eternal purpose which he accomplished in Christ Jesus our Lord. In him and

through faith in him we may approach God with freedom and confidence. I ask you, therefore, not to be discouraged because of my sufferings for you, which are your glory.

For this reason I kneel before the Father, from whom his whole family in heaven and on earth derives its name. I pray that out of his glorious riches he may strengthen you with power through his Spirit in your inner being. (Ephesians 3:10–16)

God's family is not an institution, as many have experienced it through the years of church tradition. That was never God's plan. It is to be a living, dynamic organism where each member belongs to the other.

Just as each of us has one body with many members, and these members do not all have the same function, so in Christ we who are many form one body, and each member belongs to all the others. (Romans 12:4–5)

The fact is, when we become Christians God puts us in his family. We do belong...to him and to one another.

> With many other words he warned them; and he pleaded with them, "Save yourselves from this corrupt generation." Those who accepted his message were baptized, and about three thousand were added to their number that day.
>
> They devoted themselves to the apostles' teaching and to the fellowship, to the breaking of bread and to prayer. Everyone was filled with awe, and many wonders and miraculous signs were done by the apostles. All the believers were together and had everything in common. (Acts 2:40–44)

As for Gator Goose....

When Mom was no longer there for him, my sister took Gator Goose to another pond a few miles away, hoping he

could find "goose happiness." When she went back to check on him later, he was not there. My guess is he went looking for home.

We all want to find the place we feel at home. We are not meant to live this life alone. Jesus calls us all to be in a spiritual family and have relationships with one another that help us make it all the way to heaven.

We can learn lessons about community from this goose story by Dr. Robert McNeish.

The Goose Story

Next
fall, when
you see geese
heading south for
the winter, flying along
in V formation, you might
consider what science has dis-
covered as to why they fly that way:
as each bird flaps its wings, it creates an
uplift for the bird immediately following. By
flying in V formation the whole flock adds at least
71% greater flying range than if each bird flew on its own.

People who share a
common direction and sense of community
can get where they are going more quickly and easily
because they are traveling on the thrust of one another.

When
a goose falls
out of formation,
it suddenly feels the drag
and resistance of trying to go it alone
and quickly gets back into formation to take
advantage of the lifting power of the bird in front.

If we have as much sense as a goose,
we will stay in formation
with those who are headed the same way we are.

Finding Your Place to Belong

When
the Head Goose
gets tired, it rotates back
in the wing and another goose flies point.

**It is sensible to take turns doing demanding jobs
with people or with geese flying south.**

Geese
honk from behind to
encourage those up front to keep up their speed.

What do we say when we honk from behind?

Finally,
and this is important,
when a goose gets sick, or is
wounded by gunshots and falls out
of formation, two other geese fall out with that
goose and follow it down to lend help and protection.
They stay with the fallen goose until it is able to fly, or until
it dies. Only then do they launch out on their own,
or with another formation
to catch up with their group.

**If we have the sense of a goose,
we will stand by each other
like that.**

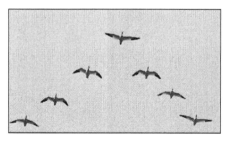

As this book closes, I pray you better know what it means to "understand Goose." I hope that you have begun your migration "home"—with Jesus at the head and with the help and support of a spiritual family around you.

Find your place in the V formation of your spiritual family. Sometimes you'll need the strength of another's up-lift or a honk from behind. Sometimes you will need to fall back, and at times you may even be able to take the lead. There will also be times you will need to slow to care for another who is wounded. We need each other to make it home. Jesus can take us there. The choice to go is yours. I close with a few of the words from one of my favorite hymns by Will Thompson.

Softly and tenderly Jesus is calling,
Calling for you and for me.
See, on the portals, He's waiting and watching;
Watching for you and for me.

Why should we linger when Jesus is pleading?
Pleading for you and for me.
Why should we linger and heed not His mercies?
Mercies for you and for me.

Come home, come home
You who are weary come home...

Supplemental Questions

Chapter One: Jesus Understands

1. Describe several circumstances or situations where you have felt "different"—as if you don't fit in or are not understood:

_____

_____

_____

2. Give an example of how this feeling affects you as you interact with those around you.

_____

_____

_____

3. Describe several circumstances where Jesus may have felt "different" and misunderstood.

_____

_____

_____

4. Read the following scriptures and describe how Jesus can offer you hope. (The Old Testament scriptures show us the heart of God, which Jesus embodied in flesh in the New Testament.)

Deuteronomy 1:29–31   Matthew 11: 28–30
Isaiah 40:11   John 10:10–11
Jeremiah 29: 11–14   John 14:23
Zephaniah 3: 17–20

_____

_____

_____

_____

_____

_____

Chapter 2: Jesus Completes Me (Jesus and Loss)

See Appendix A for further material on loss

1. List several of the most significant losses you have experienced.

   _____

   _____

   _____

2. What are some of the emotions you feel that may be related to these losses?

   _____

   _____

   _____

3. Can you describe some stages of grief to which you can relate?

   _____

   _____

   _____

4. What are some ways you have responded to your losses as you tried to fill the void?

   _____

   _____

   _____

5. How can Jesus relate to your feelings of loss? What are some ways Jesus experienced loss?

_____

_____

_____

6. Read Hebrews 2:14–18 and Hebrews 4:15.
   What difference does it make to know that someone can understand you and relate to you?

_____

_____

_____

7. Read the following scriptures and describe what Jesus is offering you that can fill your loneliness:

Matthew 28:18–20	John 10:9–10	John 11:25–26
John 4:13–14	John 10:11	John 14:6
John 6:35	John 10:14	John 15:5
John 8:12		

_____

_____

_____

Chapter 3: Jesus Chooses Me (Jesus and Rejection)

1. What are some of the ways you have felt/been rejected?

_____

_____

_____

2. What are some ways you have responded to feelings of rejection?

_____

_____

_____

3. What might it feel like to really feel accepted? Wanted?

_____

_____

_____

4. What are some ways Jesus experienced rejection?

_____

_____

_____

5. Read the following scriptures. How do they promise and reassure you that Jesus has not only chosen you, but wants a relationship with you?

Isaiah 49:14–16   John 17:9–26   Colossians 3:12
Matthew 23:37   Ephesians 1:3–6

_____

_____

_____

6. What are some promises of God that you can turn to when feeling rejected? Search through the Scriptures to find some promises of God that particularly help you, and list them here.

_____

_____

_____

7. Will you decide to accept that God really does love you and wants a relationship with you? If so, how will that fact change the way you choose to live?

_____

_____

_____

Chapter 4: Jesus Makes Me Innocent
(Jesus on Shame and Guilt)

1. How can you know if the guilt you feel is warranted, or if it is misplaced?

_____

_____

_____

2. What are some things you feel ashamed of?

_____

_____

_____

3. How does the shame and guilt you carry affect your view of yourself?

_____

_____

_____

4. What are some ways this shame and guilt affects your relationship to God and to people?

_____

_____

_____

5. Is the shame and guilt you feel from things other people have done to you your fault?
Do you really believe that these things are not your fault? If so, what difference will this make in your thinking?

_____

_____

_____

6. You can't control what happened to you. What can you control?

_____

_____

_____

7. Read the following scriptures. Describe how Jesus took on your shame and guilt so that you don't have to keep experiencing it.

Romans 5:5–11
Romans 6:3–8
1 Peter 2:22–25

_____

_____

_____

8. Read the following scriptures. What does trust in God have to do with overcoming shame?

   Psalm 25:1–5   Psalm 34:4–5   Ezekiel 18:19–20
   Psalm 31   Isaiah 53:10–12

   _____

   _____

   _____

9. Read the following scriptures and note how Jesus allows you to be/feel innocent and therefore confident:

   Psalm 103:8–18   Romans 8:1–4, 31–39
   Isaiah 1:18   1 Peter 3:21
   Acts 2:38–39   1 John 1:5–7

   _____

   _____

   _____

10. Concerning things that you have done and are ashamed of…what difference would it make in your life to not only *be* completely forgiven, but also to *feel* completely forgiven?

   _____

   _____

   _____

11. What are other scriptures you can turn to that can help you feel confident, forgiven and accepted?

_____

_____

_____

15. Will you decide to believe these scriptures, or the accusations that play as "tapes" in your mind?

_____

_____

_____

Chapter 5: Jesus Knows Me (Jesus and Identity)

1. How would you introduce yourself?
   My name is _____ and I am _____?

2. When you don't have a strong sense of your identity, how does it affect your confidence in relationships with others?

   _____

   _____

   _____

3. How does lack of confidence affect your relationship with others?

   _____

   _____

   _____

4. How can Jesus relate to you when you feel you don't fit in?

   _____

   _____

   _____

5. Read John 8:14.
   Jesus was confident of where he came from and where he was going. How did this confidence affect his daily life? How could this confidence affect your daily life?

   _____

   _____

   _____

6. Read the following scriptures. What are some of the descriptions Jesus gives you of your true identity?

2 Corinthians 2:15
Ephesians 3:17b–19
Philippians 3:20–21
Colossians 1:10–12
1 Peter 2:9

_____

_____

_____

7. Read the following scriptures. What privileges, inheritance and security do you gain by being a son or daughter of God?

John 1:12
John 14:1–4
Romans 8:38–39
Galatians 4:7
1 John 3:1–2
Revelation 17:14

_____

_____

_____

Chapter 6: Jesus Is Trustworthy
(Jesus on Intimacy and Trust)

1. What do you view as the top three life events that affect your ability to trust?

_____

_____

_____

2. How does lack of trust show itself in your life?

_____

_____

_____

3. How does lack of trust affect your ability to get close to others?

_____

_____

_____

4. What are current ways you tend to keep others at a distance?

_____

_____

_____

5. Why might it have been hard for Jesus to open up and be vulnerable with others?

_____

_____

_____

6. Is Jesus trustworthy? If so, and if you decide to trust him, what would that look like for you?

_____

_____

_____

7. Why would trusting Jesus help you be vulnerable with other people?

_____

_____

_____

8. State a decision you will make that will allow you to begin to open up to another person.

_____

_____

_____

9. Read John 15:13–15 and 2 Corinthians 6:11–13. What do these scriptures teach you about intimacy and trust?

_____

_____

_____

For further consideration:

Why does praying take intimacy and trust?

Begin reading through the Psalms, noting and learning from David's vulnerability before God.

Notice how David freely opens up his heart to God. Try writing or praying the innermost thoughts of your heart to God.

Chapter 7: Jesus Can Take the Wheel
(Jesus and Control)

1. What are ways you try to take control in your life?

_____

_____

_____

2. What fears do you have when you're not in control?

_____

_____

_____

3. Read Luke 22:39–44. What can you learn from Jesus' intense struggle to submit his will to God's will as he prayed in the garden?

_____

_____

_____

4. Read Romans 7:15–25. Try to describe the struggle for control that goes on in your life.

_____

_____

_____

5. Read the following scriptures. What are some promises God gives you to help you let go of the controls?

Psalm 139
Isaiah 55:9–11
Romans 8:9–16
Galatians 5:13–23
2 Peter 1:3–4

_____

_____

_____

Appendix A
Stages of Grief

The Kübler-Ross stages of grief, also known as the 5 stages of grief, were first outlined in 1969, when Elisabeth Kübler-Ross's book *On Death and Dying* (Simon & Schuster, 1969) was published. Her work was a reflection of the grief process of patients who had been diagnosed with terminal illness. These stages later came to be applied to other forms of significant loss, and have resonated with many. In a later book, *On Grief and Grieving,* Kübler-Ross clarifies a misunderstanding from the previous book when she states, "They [the stages] were never meant to tuck messy emotions into neat packages. They are responses to loss that many people have, but there is not a typical response to loss, as there is no typical loss."

She says these stages are tools to help us frame and identify what we may be feeling as a result of various losses in our lives. They are not stops on a linear timeline and not everyone goes through all of them. Here are the Kübler-Ross stages of grief:

1. Denial

For those who have received a diagnosis of a terminal illness, this is the initial reaction to hearing the devastating news. It is a natural defense mechanism as you are being forced to absorb the unthinkable.

"But I feel so healthy. It can't be real."

For those who have lost a loved one, the denial stage is more symbolic. You know mentally that your loved one has died, but you just can't believe it. You simply can't fathom that they will never walk through the door again.

"I can't believe she is dead."

The denial stage is the psyche's protective mechanism. It helps us absorb the tragic news at a slower rate so we are not completely overwhelmed by it.

2. Anger

Rage and resentment replace denial as the full impact of the diagnosis begins to sink in.

"This isn't fair. I didn't do anything to deserve this."

3. Bargaining

The person tries to bargain with God or a Higher Power in order to gain a longer life.

"Just let me live long enough to see my grandchild's birth." "I'll do anything if you give me a few more years."

4. Depression

In this stage the person gives up on bargaining and realizes that death is coming. It is a sad and difficult time when the person may refuse to enter into the life they have left. They must be allowed this time to mourn.

"I'm going to die, so why bother trying to live?"

5. Acceptance

The person comes to realize death is coming and is now able to find some measure of peace with the process.

"Death is coming, but I will be okay."

There are several models that vary a bit which may be helpful in looking at the grief stages. Please keep in mind that every grief journey is different. Some people go through the stages in a different order. Some stay longer in one stage and briefly in another. Different components of your life and grief situation also make the stages feel different and unique to you. *However, above all, remember that Jesus will walk with you if you let him.*

Appendix B
Shame, Guilt and Forgiveness

Read Ezekiel 18:20 and Mark 7:20–24. What do these scriptures teach you about differentiating between what is your responsibility and what is not your responsibility?

Forgiveness is basic to overcoming shame and guilt. We must ultimately seek and find forgiveness for those things that are our responsibility and offer forgiveness for wrongs done to us.

Read the following scriptures:

Genesis 50:16–17

So they sent word to Joseph saying, "Your father left these instructions before he died: 'This is what you are to say to Joseph: I ask you to forgive your brothers the sins and the wrongs they committed in treating you so badly.' Now please forgive the sins of the servants of the God of your father." When their message came to him, Joseph wept.

Matthew 6:14–15

"For if you forgive men when they sin against you, your heavenly Father will also forgive you. But if you do not forgive men their sins, your Father will not forgive your sins."

Matthew 18:21

Then Peter came to Jesus and asked, "Lord, how many times shall I forgive my brother when he sins against me? Up to seven times?"

Matthew 18:35

"This is how my heavenly Father will treat each of you unless you forgive your brother from your heart."

Mark 11:25

"And when you stand praying, if you hold anything against anyone, forgive him, so that your Father in heaven may forgive you your sins."

Luke 17:3–4

"So watch yourselves. If your brother sins, rebuke him, and if he repents, forgive him. If he sins against you seven times in a day, and seven times comes back to you and says, 'I repent,' forgive him."

Luke 23:34

Jesus said, "Father, forgive them, for they do not know what they are doing." And they divided up his clothes by casting lots.

Colossians 3:13

Bear with each other and forgive whatever grievances you may have against one another. Forgive as the Lord forgave you.

Hebrews 12:15

See to it that no one misses the grace of God and that no bitter root grows up to cause trouble and defile many.

James 3:14

But if you harbor bitter envy and selfish ambition in your hearts, do not boast about it or deny the truth.

Choosing: The Bondage of Bitterness or The Freedom of Forgiveness

The Bondage of Bitterness

1. What is bitterness?

What does bitterness look like in an individual?

_____

_____

_____

How do you know if you are bitter?

_____

_____

_____

Consider the following scriptures:

Proverbs 14:10
> Each heart knows its own bitterness,
> and no one else can share its joy.

Hebrews 12:15
> See to it that no one misses the grace of God and that no bitter root grows up to cause trouble and defile many.

Ephesians 4:31
> Get rid of all bitterness, rage and anger, brawling and slander, along with every form of malice.

Does bitterness have accompanying sins and consequences? What are they?

_____

_____

2. Read Mark 7:21–23. Where does bitterness come from?

_____

_____

_____

Do hurts, disappointments, abusive or unfair treatment make you bitter, or do they tempt you to be bitter? What is the difference?

_____

_____

_____

According to the Scriptures, who is responsible for bitterness?

_____

_____

_____

3. Read Hebrews 12:15, James 3:14 and Ephesians 4:29–32. Why does bitterness keep you in bondage?

_____

_____

_____

Who does it hurt?

_____

_____

_____

The above scriptures show that bitterness hurts many others, hurts you and results in you not being forgiven by God. It also grieves the Holy Spirit of God.

4. **Read Matthew 6:14–15. How important is it that you forgive?**

_____

_____

_____

When have you been most tempted to be bitter? How did/does it show?

_____

_____

_____

Who are you most tempted to be bitter toward?

_____

_____

_____

5. **How do you break free from bitterness?**
   a. Identify the source of your bitterness/anger/unforgiveness.

_____

_____

_____

b. Allow yourself to feel the hurt. What happens when you don't do that?

_____

_____

_____

Can you forgive someone when you don't hold them responsible? Why or why not?

_____

_____

_____

c. Confront the source of your hurt.
Read Matthew 18:15–17, for some instruction from Jesus about dealing with people who have sinned against you.

It is wise to be prayerful and to seek counsel on the most appropriate way to confront the source of your hurt. Only with prayer and the example of Jesus will you be able to decide to forgive, whether or not you receive an apology or admission of guilt from the other person. However, this must be your goal. Some have found it helpful to write a letter describing how the person's sin has hurt and affected them. It is important for you to state the hurt that has been inflicted upon you, but also to come to a point where you are able to offer forgiveness regardless of the response you receive. You may decide to deliver the letter, but it may not be advisable to do so, or even possible, if the person is no longer living or accessible. Upon completion of this difficult task, you may want to tear up or burn the letter as a remembrance and symbol of closure to this big step in your life.

d. Offer forgiveness.

Jesus' example gives us the model, and his love and strength give us the courage:

Jesus said, "Father, forgive them, for they do not know what they are doing." And they divided up his clothes by casting lots. (Luke 23:34)

Colossians 3:13 states,

Bear with each other and forgive whatever grievances you may have against one another. Forgive as the Lord forgave you.

6. **Read 1 Peter 2:23 How do you forgive? (Study the example of Jesus.)**

Jesus shows us how to forgive by his example. Perhaps Jesus' greatest temptation to sin was on the cross. Do you think Jesus was tempted with bitterness?

_____

How was he able to overcome?

_____

_____

_____

Read the following scriptures:

Psalm 103:12	1 Corinthians 13:4–7
Jeremiah 31:34	Colossians 3:13
Matthew 18:21–22	

What are some characteristics of forgiveness that will be obvious in your life?

_____

_____

_____

How can you know if you have forgiven someone from your heart?

_____

_____

_____

7. Why is it freeing to forgive?
Read Genesis 37–41. What injustices did Joseph experience?

_____

_____

_____

How do we see the freedom that forgiveness brings in this biblical example of Joseph with his brothers?

_____

_____

_____

Read Genesis 42–50. What allowed Joseph to offer forgiveness to his brothers? How did he show this forgiveness and what was the result?

_____

_____

_____

8. Who will decide if you will be enslaved to your bitterness or set free by forgiveness?
What decisions do you need to make?

_____

_____

_____

Appendix C
Who I Am In Christ

Who I Am In Christ
Biblical Truths for "Practical Beliefs"

I AM GOD'S...
- possession. (Genesis 17:8; 1 Corinthians 6:20)
- child. (John 1:12)
- handiwork. (Ephesians 2:10)
- friend. (John 15:15)
- temple. (1 Corinthians 3:16, 6:16)
- vessel. (2 Timothy 2:2)
- delight. (Zephaniah 3:17)
- soldier. (2 Timothy 2:3)
- ambassador. (2 Corinthians 5:20)
- building. (1 Corinthians 3:9)
- fellow worker. (1 Corinthians 3:9)
- minister/instrument. (1 Timothy 4:6)
- chosen. (Ephesians 1:4)
- beloved. (Romans 1:7; 2 Thessalonians 2:13)
- treasured possession. (Malachi 3:17)
- heir. (Galatians 3:29)

I HAVE BEEN...
- redeemed by the blood. (Revelation 5:9)
- set free from sin /condemnation. (Romans 8:1–2)
- set free from Satan's control. (Colossians 1:13)

- set free from Satan's kingdom. (Ephesians 2)
- chosen before foundation of world. (Ephesians 1:4)
- predestined to be like Jesus. (Ephesians 1:11)
- forgiven of all my trespasses. (Colossians 2:13)
- washed in the blood of the Lamb. (Revelation 1:5)
- given a spirit of power, love and self-discipline.
  (2 Timothy 1:7)
- given the Holy Spirit. (2 Corinthians 1:22)
- adopted into God's family. (Romans 8:15)
- justified freely by his grace. (Romans 3:24)
- given all things pertaining to life. (2 Peter 1:3)
- given great and precious promises. (2 Peter 1:4)
- given His seal of ownership. (2 Corinthians 1:22)
- given the ministry of reconciliation. (2 Corinthians 5:19)
- given access to God. (Ephesians 3:12)
- given wisdom. (Ephesians 1:8)

I AM...

- complete in him. (Colossians 2:10)
- free from sin's power. (Romans 6:14)
- sanctified. (1 Corinthians 6:11)
- made for the Master's use. (2 Timothy 2:21)
- shielded by God's power. (1 Peter 1:5)
- eternally kept in the palm of his hand. (John 10:29)
- kept from falling. (Jude 1:24)
- kept by the power of God. (1 Peter 1:5)
- not condemned. (Romans 8:1–2)
- one with the Lord. (1 Corinthians 6:17)
- on my way to heaven. (John 14:6)
- alive with Christ. (Colossians 2:13)
- seated in heavenly places. (Ephesians 1:3)
- a candle in a dark place. (Matthew 5:15)

- a city set on a hill. (Matthew 5:14)
- the salt of the earth. (Matthew 5:13)
- his sheep. (Psalm 23; Psalm 100:3; John 10:14)
- a citizen of heaven. (Ephesians 2:19)
- hidden with Christ in God. (Psalm 32:7)
- protected from the evil one. (1 John 5:18)
- secure in Christ. (John 10:28–29)
- set on a Rock. (Psalm 40:2)
- more-than-a-conqueror. (Romans 8:37)
- born again. (1 Peter 1:23)
- a victor. (1 John 5:4)
- healed by his stripes. (Isaiah 53:6)
- covered by the blood of Jesus. (Revelation 12:11; 1 Peter 1:19)
- sheltered under his wing. (Psalm 91:4)
- resting in the shadow of the Almighty. (Psalm 91:1)

I HAVE...
- access to the Father. (Romans 5:2)
- a home in heaven waiting for me. (John 14:1–2)
- everything I need. (Philippians 4:19)
- a living hope. (1 Peter 1:3)
- an anchor to my soul. (Hebrews 6:19)
- a hope that is firm and secure. (Hebrews 6:19)
- the mind of Christ. (1 Corinthians 2:16)
- boldness and access. (Hebrews 10:19)
- peace with God. (Romans 5:1)
- love, joy, peace, patience, kindness, gentleness, faithfulness and self control. (Galatians 5:22–23)

I CAN...

- do all things through Christ. (Philippians 4:13)
- find mercy and grace to help. (Hebrews 4:16)
- come boldly to the throne of grace. (Hebrews 4:16)
- quench all the fiery darts. (Ephesians 6:16)
- pray always and everywhere. (Luke 21:36)
- chase a thousand. (Joshua 23:10–11)
- defeat (overcome) the enemy. (Revelation 12:11)
- crush Satan under foot. (Romans 16:20)
- always have a way of escape. (1 Corinthians 10:13)

I CANNOT...

- be separated from God's love. (Romans 8:35–39)
- be shaken. (Psalm 16:8)
- be charged or accused. (Romans 8:33)
- be condemned. (1 Corinthians 11:32)

Made in the USA
Charleston, SC
03 September 2011